Williamsburg
Eyewitness to History
Series

WILLIAMSBURG EYEWITNESS TO HISTORY SERIES

The Journal and Letters of Philip Vickers Fithian
The Journal of Major George Washington
The Journal of John Harrower

THE JOURNAL OF JOHN HARROWER

The Journal of
JOHN HARROWER

An Indentured Servant in the
Colony of Virginia, 1773–1776

Edited, with an Introduction, by

EDWARD MILES RILEY

ILLUSTRATED BY FRITZ KREDEL

COLONIAL WILLIAMSBURG
Williamsburg, Virginia

Distributed by
HOLT, RINEHART AND WINSTON, INC.
New York

To
Annette, Patsy, Kathy
Miles and Clay

Acknowledgements

MANY persons have assisted me in editing the journal and in writing the introduction. To all of them I am grateful. The following have been notably helpful: Mr. George H. S. King of Fredericksburg, who identified many of the obscure individuals mentioned in the journal, who suggested subjects for the footnotes, and who helped in many other ways; Dr. E. G. Swem, Librarian Emeritus of the College of William and Mary, who read the introduction and notes and gave me much valuable advice; Mr. William J. Van Schreeven and the staff of the Archives Division, Virginia State Library; Mr. John M. Jennings and the staff of the Virginia Historical Society; Mr. James A. Servies and the staff of the Library of the College of William and Mary; and my colleagues of Colonial Williamsburg—Dr. E. P. Alexander, Mr. J. R. Short, and Mr. J. J. Walklet of the Division of Interpretation; Mr. Paul Buchanan of the Architectural Department; Dr. J. E. Selby, Dr. Jane Carson, Miss Kay Taylor, and Mrs. Louann Witcofski of the Research Department—for constant aid and helpful criticism.

EDWARD M. RILEY

Contents

ILLUSTRATIONS

Introduction

MARCH 10, 1774: Standing on the deck of the westward-bound *Planter*, a merchantman in the Virginia trade, John Harrower gazed at the Cornish cliffs of Land's End as the coast of England drifted slowly out of sight. Forty years of age, he had now made the most critical decision of his life—to leave his wife and children behind and continue to search for the means to support them. Three months' fruitless pursuit of employment in Scotland and England, when both were prostrated by depression, had left him with but a single alternative to destitution. He accepted it—in the form of a contract called an indenture. In exchange for ocean passage and an uncertain future in a raw new country he had pledged the next four years of both his labor and his independence. If there was a momentary sagging of his Scottish spirit at the thought of the choice he had made, Harrower registered no despair in his journal. The entry for the day was brief and unreflective: the sails were full, and accompanied by a brigantine bound for Jamaica the *Planter* plowed out into the Atlantic at 7 ½ knots.

John Harrower was not unique. His journal is. He alone of the great army of indentured servants who came to colonial Virginia has left us a record of his daily life. Like the slaves, indentured servants made up a large segment of the population and did most of the manual work, but as individuals they are generally anonymous.[1]

The account opens on December 6, 1773, when the impoverished merchant left his home in Lerwick, a village in the northerly Shetland Islands of Scotland, and began his travels "in search of business." Financially he was "so straitned that nothing but money upon Interest for some Considerable time" could have rescued him from becoming, as he quietly put it, "personally exposed."[2]

Escape from perennial grinding poverty in Scotland was the greatest single reason behind what James Boswell called "a rage for emigration" in the 1770's.[3] For many years tenant farmers, shopkeepers, and Harrower's fellow merchants had endured oppressive rents levied by the landed proprietors. In the Shetlands, Crown rents were farmed out to the highest bidder in each parish. Chamberlains of the Crown and agents of the landlords were the instruments of extortion. To avoid this dismal and penniless future, some young men went off to sea, though not to fish; the fishing industry was severely taxed to pay the ministers' salaries. Other men set out to find employment in England or on the continent or, failing that, signed an indenture for the colonies.[4]

The panic of 1772 intensified the already desperate economic crisis. But Harrower expected to find work in England. At worst, he "did not intend going further than Holland" in search of temporary relief. Yet this capable man found that he was unable to obtain passage to Holland or to find any kind of employment in the seaports of Scotland and eastern England. Sorely disappointed, Harrower walked the eighty long miles from Portsmouth to London, paying for his meager subsistence en route by gradually selling off his capital—a small supply of the famous Shetland stockings. A stranger to London, he wandered through that great city "like a blind man without a guide." Appeals to merchants and shipmasters for work brought only shrugs. Answering advertisements in the newspapers proved fruitless, for hundreds of unemployed were starving and many "good people" were begging. His integrity and Scots pride would not allow Harrower to beg, but bread and cheese became his scanty and unvarying fare. Alone "in a garret room . . . frendless and forsaken" he found relief from anxiety and hunger in prayer and confided in his journal:

> I'll unto God my prayer make,
>   to him my case make known;
> And hopes he will for Jesus sake,
>   Provide for me and soon.

Finally, "reduced to the last shilling," he "was oblidged to engage to go to Virginia for four years."

For the next sixteen weeks and six days, he was to live on the *Planter*. His description of life on board a ship carrying indentured servants is graphic and detailed. He was quickly recognized by the captain, David Bowers, as a responsible person of strong character. When some of the servants, before the actual sailing, threatened to mutiny over the allowance of food, Captain Bowers asked Harrower to "stand by the mate if there arose any disturbance among the rest of the servants." During the long voyage, he nursed the numerous sick passengers and crew, often throughout the night, and while the chief mate was ill, he kept the ship's journal and log.

When the *Planter* anchored at Fredericksburg, Virginia, Captain Bowers recommended him strongly to William Anderson, the merchant responsible for the sale of the servants' indentures. Anderson reserved Harrower's indenture until Fair Day, when the gentry would be in town for the races. Thus Harrower was able to see the town while he waited and to describe it in his journal.

Although he had been a merchant, he took little notice of the flourishing commercial activity at Fredericksburg and its sister port of Falmouth. Situated at the head of navigation on the Rappahannock River, the towns formed a center of trade for the rapidly developing Piedmont. Here were located the large mercantile establishments of William Allason, John Glassell, Roger Dixon, James Hunter, and James Ritchie. Many of the merchants operated subsidiary stores throughout the Piedmont and the Valley of Virginia. This concentration of mercantile activity, with its numerous stores and warehouses, gave Fredericksburg a bustling commercial atmosphere as well as a gay and opulent air.[5]

The fertile land in the Fredericksburg area had attracted many wealthy planters, such as William Fitzhugh of Chatham and Mann Page of Mannsfield, who added luster to the social life of the town. At the time of Harrower's arrival Fredericksburg was a leading center in Virginia for the popular sport of horse racing. Concerts, balls, and theatrical productions made it also a focal point of cultural life in northern Virginia.[6]

Among the gentlemen and ladies who drove into town for the Fair was Anderson's friend, Colonel William Daingerfield, in search of a tutor. Anderson introduced Harrower to him, the two men "imediatly agreed," and the new tutor could record with great satisfaction: "my Indenture for four years was then delivered him and he was to send for me the next day. At the same time ordred to get all my dirty Cloaths of every kind washed at his expence in Toun; at night he sent me five shillings on board by Capt. Bowers to keep my pocket."

Harrower's employer belonged to the branch of an old Tidewater family that had moved into the fertile region along the Rappahannock River in the seventeenth century and established a prominent position in its political and social life.[7] William, the eldest son, inherited his father's plantation in New Kent County. Educated in England, he was well trained to assume the duties and responsibilities of his position. His public career began in 1762 when he was chosen a vestryman for Blisland Parish, and a few years later he was named a county justice of the peace and colonel of the militia.[8] As his political life advanced, financial problems absorbed more and more of his time. On the fatherly advice of the London merchant Samuel Athawes, he tried to improve both the quality of his tobacco crops and his business efficiency, but with little success. Perhaps he ignored Athawes' warning against the tendency of Virginia planters to "over value their incomes, & live up to their suppositions without providing against Calamities accidents &c."[9]

Discouraged in New Kent, Colonel Daingerfield, a few years before employing Harrower, moved his residence.[10] His wife Sarah had inherited from her father, Lawrence Taliaferro, a 1,300-acre plantation about seven miles below Fredericksburg.[11] Here, on a high bluff overlooking the Rappahannock, Daingerfield built his mansion Belvidera in 1769 or 1770.[12]

To the Scots tutor the plantation must have resembled a small village. Kitchen, laundry, dairy, smokehouse, and schoolhouse were grouped around the mansion house, while barns, corncribs, slave quarters, stables, and shops were situated on the periphery. Large fields beyond the buildings were planted in wheat and corn. On the river bank stood the customary wharf.

The plantation, the house, and its furnishings reflected the position of the owner. Belvidera could not compare with the princely domains of the Pages, the Fitzhughs, and the Spotswoods. Yet Daingerfield concentrated all his efforts on the management of the plantation.[13] Following the example of other tobacco planters who were solving the problems of soil exhaustion and unsatisfactory marketing conditions by substituting grains as money crops, he planted his fields at

Belvidera in wheat and Indian corn.[14] His farming methods excited the interest of the tutor, who devoted much space in the journal and letters to the details of planting, cultivating, harvesting, threshing, storing, and shipping grain.

The atmosphere at Belvidera was one of work and business with little time for the less practical things of life. There were few visitors and no elegant dances, banquets, or other traditional diversions of the gentry. Harrower's place in the household was not the usual position of an indentured servant. He ate at his master's table, shared in the enjoyment of visitors, and frequently went with the family to church, barbecues, or boating and fishing parties. Yet he always waited for an invitation from his master and never took his participation in family affairs for granted. Comfortable and grateful, he informed his wife, "I never lived a genteel regulare life untill now," and assured her, "I design to see & prepare a way for you all in this Country how soon I am able."

Although one of Daingerfield's overseers found him "a fickle Master to do with," Harrower apparently won his master's respect and their relationship was always warm and friendly. When the Colonel had difficulties with overseers, he would ask the tutor to assume additional duties. Small gifts were frequent, and occasionally the master would suggest that the tutor go to Fredericksburg to watch a militia muster, attend horse races, or visit friends. There was never any disagreement to mar the friendship of the two men. In fact, when Mrs. Daingerfield became angry with Harrower for punishing her son William, the Colonel came to the tutor's defense.

Daingerfield's intelligent interest in the education of his children reflected a basic concern of the Virginia gentry. To them ignorance was a disgrace, for, as one planter put it, an uneducated person would be "noways capable of the management of his own affairs & unfit for any Gentleman's conversation, & therefore a Scandalous person, & a Shame to his Relations, not having one single qualification to recommend him."[15]

Harrower's unusual privileges indicated the importance of his work and his superior personality traits. Another Virginia tutor, Jonathan Boucher, had only contempt for colleagues like Harrower. He complained in 1773 that

at least two thirds of the little education we receive are derived from instructors, who are either INDENTURED SERVANTS, OR TRANS-

PORTED FELONS. Not a ship arrives either with redemptioners or convicts, in which schoolmasters are not regularly advertised for sale, as weavers, tailors, or any other trade; with little difference, that I can hear of, excepting perhaps that the former do not usually fetch so good a price as the latter.[16]

Scotsmen invited special condemnation. Philip Vickers Fithian, tutor at Nomini Hall, that same year explained that it had been the custom in Virginia "heretofore to have all their Tutors, and Schoolmasters from Scotland, tho' they begin to be willing to employ their own Countrymen." He later recorded that his master, Robert Carter, preferred American-trained tutors for his children "on account of pronunciation in the English Language."[17] Another Virginian expressed his dislike of the Scottish dialect even more forcefully when he said that "the usual wages here for a Latin master from Scotland is £20 a year, but they commonly teach the children the Scotch dialect which they never can wear off."[18]

Like other private tutors, Harrower was encouraged to accept additional pupils from nearby plantations. Since the fees paid by the parents belonged to the tutor, this custom provided a source of independent income especially welcome to an indentured servant. Colonel Daingerfield even "rode through the neighbouring Gentlemen & Planters in order to procure scollars." Later, after the tutor's reputation became known, his services were requested by a number of interested parents. One of his students was a young carpenter, Thomas Brooks, who learned writing and arithmetic at nights and on Sundays. Harrower also taught writing to Lucy Gaines, the young housekeeper at Belvidera, and instructed some of the slaves in the catechism. Perhaps his most unusual pupil was John Edge, a young deaf mute—one of the first in America to receive formal instruction.[19]

Some insight into Harrower's regular teaching methods can be found in the journal. In a letter to his wife shortly after assuming his duties, he noted that he had to teach "in the English method" which he found "aquard" at first but "now quite easy." Furthermore, he was "obliged to talk english" the best he could, for Mrs. Daingerfield spoke "nothing but high english," and the Colonel had received his education in England. Undoubtedly he meant that he was persuaded by Colonel and Mrs. Daingerfield to modify his Scots accent. Harrower's customary spelling certainly indicates a broad accent.[20]

Though he lived in Virginia during momentous times, Harrower devoted little space in his journal to the events leading to the American Revolution. Latest advices were mentioned, mainly in letters to Shetland, but he was remote from the scenes of action, and life at Belvidera went on as usual with little notice of political developments. Furthermore, the tutor was absorbed in other interests—his pupils, the love affair between the overseer and the housekeeper, the cost of articles of clothing and of rum, and visits with friends. The journal is, after all, the account of a plain and simple man in a lowly position, not the thoughtful analysis of a statesman or philosopher. It records vividly the many details of daily life on an eighteenth-century plantation in Tidewater Virginia with little regard for the changing world outside.

When the journal ends abruptly in July, 1776, Harrower was well and happy but in less than a year he was dead.[21] The cause of his death cannot be determined beyond his widow's sad statement in her letter to Colonel Daingerfield that "diseases of that kind baffles all the power of medicine." Ann Harrower also noted with deep appreciation that her "late dear husband in his different letters to me had given me such an oppinion of your kind dispositions to him, as gives me no reason to doubt but that all possible Care has been taken of him in his last illness in your Hospitable Family. . . ." The tutor's fondest desire was to bring his wife and family to Virginia, and he had accumulated the sum of £70 for this purpose. The dream was not to be realized, and he died at the early age of 44 years without seeing his family again.

Even before his death, Harrower forecast coming disaster for his patron. On Christmas Day, 1775, he noted that the Colonel had returned from a trip to his New Kent quarter without receiving "one Shilling" from that plantation. Two years after making this disappointing journey Daingerfield advertised his land in New Kent for sale, but no purchaser came forward.[22]

The Daingerfield fortunes improved somewhat in the fall of 1781. Dr. Arthur Lee, while visiting his cousin William Fitzhugh at Chatham, near Fredericksburg, wrote in September that "Colonel Dangerfield and his family are well; and he has touched some hard money from the French, for his hay, which being unusual is very delightful."[23]

This happy situation was temporary. By the fall of 1782, his troubles—whether real or fancied—had reached a crisis, and the New Year brought no relief.[24] Greatly distressed and agitated, Colonel Daingerfield made his will on January 4, 1783.[25] Early the next day, a Sunday, he and Colonel Bland rode to General Spotswood's home for breakfast. Here they parted and Daingerfield set out alone "down the Country." Two weeks later a Fredericksburg lawyer, James Mercer, recorded the sudden end of the story in these words: ". . . can you believe it? Colo. Dangerfield cut his Throat at New Castle last week & is now no more! I really shall be afraid of a . . . Knife for a month to come."[26]

For more than a century John Harrower's journal remained unpublished. During that time the manuscript was preserved with the papers of the Corbin family of Moss Neck, Caroline County, and Farley Vale, King George County. The book in which the journal is written is a small quarto volume (about 6 x 8 inches) bound in vellum and containing at present 144 pages (Harrower omitted page 95). Originally it contained more, but, according to Corbin family tradition, the missing pages were used to cover jelly glasses some time during the nineteenth century.

At the turn of the last century the journal was on deposit with the Virginia Historical Society where it was called to the attention of that distinguished historian, Dr. J. Franklin Jameson, by Mrs. Sally Nelson Robins, the assistant librarian. After making a careful copy of the manuscript, he published excerpts in the October, 1900, issue of the *American Historical Review*. In making selections from the journal for publication, Dr. Jameson made "necessary omission of portions not now interesting," but with his customary editorial skill he preserved the continuity of the journal. Nevertheless, much of the colorful detail of Harrower's account was sacrificed; for example, the fascinating love affair of the overseer and the housekeeper was completely omitted.

Subsequently, the manuscript of the journal, together with the letters and accounts of Richard Corbin (1708–1790), receiver-general of Virginia, and of his children were placed on deposit with Colonial Williamsburg by the Corbin family. The widow of Matthew Maury Corbin, Mrs. Edwin E. Kimball of Schenectady, New York, and their two sons, Messrs. Spotswood Wellford Corbin and James McHenry Corbin, generously granted permission to publish the journal.

In this edition the manuscript journal is printed for the first time in its entirety. A note written by the unfortunate housekeeper under the instruction of Harrower, and Ann Harrower's revealing letter to

Colonel Daingerfield after the death of her husband have been added to the manuscript. A copy of the original list of the indentured servants who sailed with Harrower on board the *Planter* also has been appended to the journal.

In preparing the present edition for publication the editor has followed scrupulously the original text of the manuscript except that certain typographical changes have been made for improved readability. Harrower's spelling, grammar, and syntax are preserved. A few slips of the pen are corrected by bracketed letters, or by notes, and inadvertent repetitions of words, such as *and and*, are silently corrected. His capitalization and punctuation are unchanged and lower-case letters are usually retained as in the original, except that all sentences in the printed text begin with capitals and end with periods. Geographical place names and personal names with the titles attached to them have been capitalized. Abbreviations and contractions as, for example, *Mr.* or *Comr.* (for *Master* or *Commander* of a ship), are usually retained, but those not easily recognized by modern readers are given in full. All superscript letters, used commonly to indicate contractions, are expanded without notice in the printed text; for example, *wt.* to *with*, *Edr.* to *Edinburgh*, *on bd.* to *on board, blls.* to *barrels.* When missing or unintelligible words are supplied by the editor, conjectural readings are indicated by a question mark inside the brackets. Bracketed and italicized numbers, such as [*Page 1st*], indicate the pagination of the original manuscript.

Particoular Acco.t of every day's
Transactions since I left my own house
On the 6.th Dec.r 1773. ———— &
Also any remarkable occurancys
either by sea or land & ———— &
By
John Harrower

JJ smiths account £9 : 12.

Facsimile of John Harrower's title page

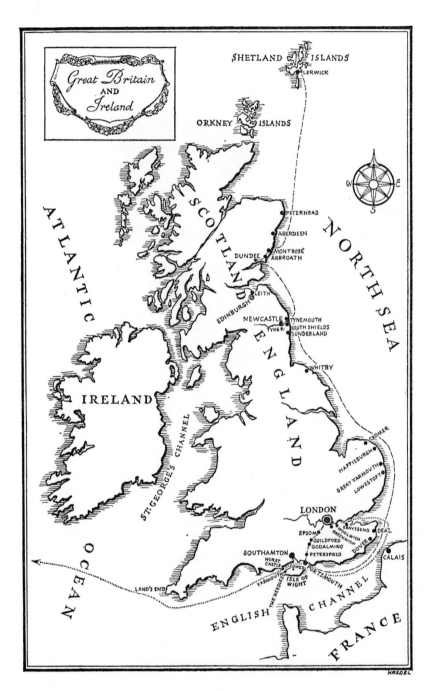

Great Britain
AND
Ireland

SHETLAND ISLANDS
LERWICK

ORKNEY ISLANDS

SCOTLAND

PETERHEAD
ABERDEEN
MONTROSE
DUNDEE ARBROATH

LEITH

EDINBURGH
NEWCASTLE TYNEMOUTH
TYNE SOUTH SHIELDS
SUNDERLAND

WHITBY

ATLANTIC

NORTH SEA

IRELAND

ENGLAND

ST. GEORGE'S CHANNEL

CROMER
HAPPISBURGH
GREAT YARMOUTH
LOWESTOFT

LONDON
WOOLWICH GRAVESEND
EPSOM GREENWICH DEAL
GUILDFORD
GODALMING DOVER
PETERSFIELD
SOUTHAMTON CALAIS
HURST
CASTLE
YARMOUTH PORTSMOUTH
THE NEEDLES COWES
ISLE OF
WIGHT
LAND'S END

OCEAN

ENGLISH CHANNEL

FRANCE

KREDEL

2

Journal

MUNDAY 6TH. DECR. 1773

This morning I left my house[1] and Family at 4 O Clock in order to travel in search of business and imediatly went on board a sloop ready to saile for Leith, Oconachie Mr. and at 5 O Clock he sailed Accordingly with the wind at N. At this time I am Master of no more Cash but 8d½ and stockins[2] &ca. to the amount of £3 Str. or thereabout, a small value indeed to traviel with.

TUESDAY 7TH

At sea the wind at N.N.E. At 6 pm passed Peterhead in a verry hard squale of wind.

WEDNESDAY 8TH

At 7 AM got a fish Boat along side, belonging to the town of Montrose and they agreed to put Mr. Barclays two sons and me ashore at Montrose for 2/6 Str. and after giving Mr. Oconachie ½ Anker[3] of butter which cost me 10/6 Str. for my passage, we put off, and landed at 8 AM. At 3 pm Mr. Barclays two sons Vizd. Pattr. & Robt.[4] set out for Aberdeen on foot. This day I was obliged to Borrow from Robert Barclay 5/ Str. which I am still due him. I stayed here all night and loged at the house of one Mr. Grahame a Taylor by trade, and was weel used at a reasonable expence.

[*Page 2d.*]   THURSDAY 9TH.

In the morning sold to a recruiting Serjant in the house 3 pair Stockins for 6/ Str. At 11 AM left Montrose and crossed the water Esk and set out for Arbroath carring my Box and bundle on my back, and at night came to Chance Inn Mid-way twixt Aberbroahick and Montrose where I loged.

FREIDAY 10TH.

Came to Aberbroathick at noon it being 4 Miles from Chance Inn. This afternoon I sold one pair Stockns. to a Mercht. here at 3/ Str. and loged all night at the house of on[e] Milne a Brewer & publican.

SATURDAY 11TH.

This morning I enquired here if there was any ship Bound for Holland or Newcastle but found there was none. I then set out for Dundee, and on the road I spoke with Lord Panmuir who is Colonel of the Regt. of Scotch Grays at present; his Brother Baron Maull[5] is at present Lord chief Barron of Exchequer at Edinburgh. This night I loged on the road at a pleace called Brigend in the house of one Caird.

SUNDAY 12TH

At no Church this day; & Nothing remarcable.

MUNDAY 13TH.

At 9 AM set out for Dundee where I aravied at 1 pm and put up at the house of one Robt. Blyth. This day on the road I called at a house for a bottle of ale, and was informed that a man who hade [*Page 3d.*] Lodged some time in the house hade on the 12 Inst. brock open another logers Chest & stole £15. 5 Str. and a silver watch and was got clear off with it.

There being no Vessel here Bound for Holland I this afternoon agreed with one Wm. Bell Mr. of a sloop for my passage to Newcastle at 5/ Str.

TUESDAY 14TH.

This day the wind S.E. which [is] contrary for us. In the afternoon I sold 6 pair stockins for 18/6 Str. In the evening gave out some shirts &ca. to wash.

WEDNESDAY 15TH.

Wind at S.E. Sold 2 pair of stockins at 5/3 Str. and bartred 3 pair which cost me 7/ Str. for two Table Cloaths 5/4 by 5/4 and 2/6 in Cash.

THURSDAY 16TH.

Wind at S.S.E. In the forenoon gave out my Short Coat to mend and keept the house all day it being a heavy rain and blowing verry hard all day. In the evining received my short Coat from the Taylor & paid him 6d. for mending it, at same time bought from him some old silver lace at 6d.

FREIDAY 17TH

Wind at E. blowing hard, with heavy rain.

SATURDAY 18TH

Wind at E.N.E. blowing verry hard with heavy rain. Sold one pair Stockins at 1/6 Str. in the afternoon sold my lace I bought 16 Inst. at 1/ Str. and bought 1 Cart slive buttons at 9d. and one Cart at 4d. Same night I sold one pair of the 9d. Cart at 5d.

[*Page 4th.*]   SUNDAY 19 DECR. 1773

Wind at E.S.E. blowing hard with rain. I went to the new Church in the forenoon Lecktour I Cor: 14 Cha; and 26 verse; Text was in Rom: I Chap: 16 verse. At same Church in the afternoon & his text was 89 Psal: 47 & 48 verses. At 5 pm went to the Methodists meeting where they were so throng I cou'd get no farther than the door, his text was in Mathew where our *Saviour* Commanded the unclean spirits to come out of the man who met him among the tombs.

MUNDAY 20TH.

Wind at E.N.E. with heavy rain & wind; nothing remarcable.

TUESDAY 21ST.

Wind and weather as yesterday. All this day employed in mending my Stockins.

WEDNESDAY 22D.

Wind at N.E. dry weather. Went to Church at 10 AM Text 3d. Gal: & 10 verse. When I came home gave out my velveret Britches to mend, and Bought some old silver lace at 6d. and sold it same day at 9½. Last night my Landlady got quite drunk, and did set her husband & Daughter in order with Swearing & Scolding.

THURSDAY 23D.

Wind at N.E.B.N. dry weather. Bought 2 pair pinchback Buckles at 10d. per pair, 1 pair steel plated with silver at 1/6d. per pair and 1 pair pinchback plated with silver at 1/10d. per. Same day sold the steel plated pair at 2/1d. Str. and 1 pair of the pinchback at 1/6 Str. to a passanger bound for London.

[*Page 5*]   FREIDAY 24TH. DECR. 1773

Wind at N.N.E. dry weather, but a verry heavy sea on the Bar. Sailed the Swallow Spmack for the Granada Islands; also the Athol Smak for London.

SATURDAY 25TH.

Wind at E.N.E. Both the Smacks in the River yet & not got over the bar.

SUNDAY 26TH.

Wind at E.N.E. Both the Smacks in the River still. Went to Church at 10 AM Text 1st Chap 2d. Timy. and 10 Verse latter part of the Verse; Went to Church at 2 pm Text 63 Chap. Isaiah 1st. verse latter part.

MUNDAY 27TH.

Wind at S.E. with heavy rain. Both the Smacks in the River yet. This evening it being St. Johns night the Free Masons made a verry grand procession through the high street.[6] They began at 6 pm and it was 11 pm before the last loge hade done. They were attended by a party of the Grandideers who carried their flambows, and each Loge walked seperatly, they being three.

TUESDAY 28TH.

Wind at E. fine weather. This day I once thought of engaging with the Mr. of the Elizabeth Brigantine bound for North Carolina but the thoughts of being so far from my family prevented me. At noon the wind came all round to the N.V.[7] and then Mr. began to make ready as fast as possible for sailing.

[*Page 6th.*]　　　WEDNESDAY 29 DECR. 1773

At 2 AM left my Loging having been here 16 days and my method of living was as follows, Vizt. for Breackfast ½ d. worth of bread, ½ d. worth of Cheese and a bottle of ale at 1d. For dinner ½ d. worth of bread, ½ d. worth of Broath, 1d. worth of Meat & a bottle of ale at 1d. & the same for supper as for breackfast, and 1d. a night for my bedd. On leaving my logings at the time above mentioned I went on board the sloop Williams; Wm. Bell Mr. for Newcastle, and he imediately hauled out of the harbour and made saile with the wind at N.N.V. At 9 pm was obliged to ly too for the tide on Tynemouth bar; at midnight bore away for the Bar and got weel over it.

THURSDAY 30TH.

At 1 AM we passed by Shiels and went up the River Tyne, and at 2 AM made fast to Newcastle Key, we having been no more than 24 hours from Dundee here 3 of which we lay too. At 9 AM I went

ashore to Newcastle in Compy. with Mr. Bell & 5 others who were
passangers along with me, and after drinking a English poynt of ale
a piece I enquired at the Pilots & others if there was any Vessel presently at Newcastle bound for Holland but found there was none. At
same time was informed that Sunderland was a more proper pleace to
look out for a Ship bound there. At 10 AM went on board the Sloop
and payed my passage and imediatly after went on board a Wherrie
for Shiels [*Page 7th*] Which cost me but 2d. for my passage tho the
distance be 7 Miles, and aravied there at noon and put up at the house
of one Mr. Boynton a Shipowner in North Shiels. After dinner I
called for Capt. Hodgson who Command the Royal Exchange Greenland Ship & enquired at him if he knew of any Ship bound for Holland, but there was none. Soon after he went over to South Shiels with
me, and enquired there bout to no purpose. But was also told that they
used the Hollands trade more from Sunderland then any other pleace,
and advised me to go there.

Capt. Hodgson goes to Greenland next season in the John and Ann
from Whiteby. He hade two large whales on board this season when
he lost his Ship in the Ice which was owing to his Chief Mate he having the watch upon deck.

FREIDAY 31ST.

Wind at N. A verry heavy fall of Snow all last night and blowing
and snowing verry hard all this day which stops me from setting foreward to Sunderland.

SATURDAY 1ST. JANY. 1774

Wind at V. fair. After Breackfast paid my lodging which cost me
6d. for dinner, four pence for supper, four pence for Breackfast and
2d. for my Bedd. At 9 AM I crossed the River for South Shiels where
I imidiatly met with the Sunderland Carrier and [*Page 8th.*] Agreed
with him to carrie my box and bundle to Sunderland for 6d. the distance being 7 Miles. At 10 AM I sat out from South Shiels on foot and
aravied at Sunderland at noon, the snow was verry deep Just now all
over the Country. At 2 pm the carrier aravied and after dinner he
went over the river with me to South Sunderland to look out for a
vessell bound for Holland, but all our enquiry was to no purpose for
we was informed that none would go to Holland Soon as they were

sure the rivers were all frozen up there; But was informed that one hade sailed on Wednesday last so that I mis'd her by 3 days.

SUNDAY 2D.

Wind at N.E Blowing & Snowing verry hard all day which made me keep the house.

MUNDAY 3D.

This day snowing verry hard. Wind at N.N.E. at 9 AM went out to see if I cou'd sell any Stockins, but returned again at 10 AM without selling any; I then paid my bedd for 2 nights which cost me 2d. each night. At same time sent out for ½ worth of bread & 1d. worth of Cheese for my breackfast, and I found both bread & Cheese far less for the money than at Dundee. Yesterday I neither eat nor drank any thing all day but my dinner which cost me 6½ and Just now I am Master of no more Cash than 1/ ½d. and when I shall get more God only knows. At 11 AM Crossed the river to South Sunderland and Called to see Wm. Scollay,[8] [*Page 9*] But was told he was not at home. After that I traviled the Toun untill 2 pm in which time I sold three pair of Stockins for four shillings & four pence which was eight pence less than they cost me in Zetland. I then returned home and bought 1d. worth of bread, 1d. worth of cheese & 1d. worth of small beer which served me for dinner & supper.

TUESDAY 4TH.

Wind at V. clear weather, and verry hard frost. Still looking out for a ship bound for Holland. Sold a few pearles I hade at 1/ they being now of no value. This day I seed plenty of fresh haddock and midling Codd brought ashore here, & one verry large ling; the haddock sold about 1d a piece. In the afternoon I bought two verry small Codd for ½d which with ½ worth of butter & 1d. worth of bread servid me for dinner and supper.

WEDNESDAY 5TH.

Wind & weather as yesterday. This afternoon I heard of a Brigantine called the Nancy ready load for Holland, & that she always used that trade.

THURSDAY 6TH.

Wind at S. and a verry gentle thaw. At 8 AM I went to Warmouth
and spacke with Mr. George Lacen [Lawson?] Comr. of the Nancy
Brigantine, who informed me, that [*Page 10th*] he himself was not
sure where he was to go, But that I might speacke to Mr. John Taylor
the Owner which I immediately did and he told me, that if the Rivers
was open the Nancy would go to Holland if not probably to London
and that I was extreamly welcome to my passage. I then waited on
Mr. Lacen & acquanted him of the same, and imediatly put my trunk
and bundle on board. I then took a Solitarry walk in North Sunderland Church Yard, where I found the following verse on the grave
Stone of Thomas Fosters—

> Why do we murn departing friends,
>   Or Shake at deaths Alarms;
> I'ts but the voice that Jesus sends,
>   To call them to his Arms.—

I pray may we all walk so in this life, that we may be called by Jesus
to his Arms at death.

The toune of Sunderland is divided by the river Vear, But that
part of it on the south side of the River is by far the largest and hand-
somest.

FREIDAY 7TH.

Got out of bedd at 6 AM this morning. At 8 AM went. At 9 AM they
began to haul out of the harbour & came to an Anchor in the Roads
at 10 AM and lay in the road untill four keels of Coals was put on
board, each Keel being Twenty Tun, and they were all on board.
[*Page 11th*] By half an houre past noon. At 1 pm got under saile with
the wind at N.B.E. with a verry high sea runing a great deall of which
she shipped all this afternoon. Steered untill midnight S.S.E.

SATURDAY 8TH.

Wind at N.N.V. fine moderate weather. Steering in S.B.V. to sight
the land; at same time the following verse writen on the grave stone
of an English Admiral was told me—

> Tho Boreas blasts
> And Neptunes vaves
>   have toss'd me too and froo

> Yet once again by Gods decree
> I'm harbour'd here below;
> Where I now at anchor ly
> with many of our fleet
> Yet once again we must set saile
> Our Admiral Christ to meet.

As I am now sailing on the sea; May the great God who made the same and all things out of nothing grant that I and all mankind may meet Christ in mercy.

SUNDAY 9TH.

Wind at N.N.E. Sleety showres. At 8 AM we was abreast of Cromar close in with the land steering S.B.E. I seed Hesbury Church[9] as we passed. About 2 pm went throu Yarmouth roads. The toune [*Page 12th*] Appears to be large and popolous. At 6 pm was two Leagues south from Leystaff [Lowestoft] roads.

MUNDAY 10TH.

This morning at 8 AM was close in withe the N. foreland. At 10 AM went throu the Downs where I seed two East India ships lying outward bound. About noon passed by Dover and seed Dover Castle & the Hils or Clifs of Cailes in France all at the same time. Seed a large Dutch Ship who hade lost her Main and fore masts and hade got up Jury Masts. She was steering the same course that we was.

TUESDAY 11TH.

At 8 AM seed the Isle of Wight. The reason of our going to the westward was our speacking with two ships on Sunday 9th. The one came from Holland who hade hard getting out by reason of the frost there and the other from Portsmouth who told us that Coals was giving a verry high price there. At 10 AM passed by ten saile of Men of War lying at Spithead & at 11 AM came to an Anchor in Portsmouth harbour. At noon I went ashore with Capt. Lacen to Portsmouth he to sell his coals and me to look out for a ship bound for Holland, or for bussines, neither of which I could find and as Capt. Lacen was offred no more but 23/ Str. per Chalder he sold none, but set out for South Hamptoun by land. I stayed seeing the Toun of Portsmouth untill 4 pm. [*Page 13th*] It is well fortifyed all round and the Streets pretty regular and clean. But no trade in it, now in peaceable times. This day fine clear weather. But a verry hard frost. I then returned on board the Nancy where I stayed all night.

WEDNESDAY 12TH.

This morning fine clear weather but hard frost. I waited on board untill three pm for Capt. Lacens returning. But when I found he did not I left a letter of thanks to him for his favours shown me, for he would take no passage money from me. Besides that he used me like a Brother making me sleep and eat with himself; I then went ashore and immediatly set out for London with no more cash in my pocket 1/8/2d. Str.—I pray, May God provide more for me and for all who are in Strait.—Immediatly as I left Portsmouth I fell into Compy. and conversaition on the road to whome I sold two pair of Stockins at 4/6d. it being the price they cost me in Zetland. I traveled four Miles this afternoon and lodged all night at Post down brige and the House hade a Battery of twelve Canon round it. Here I supped on eight Oisters at 1d. and ½ worth of Bread, with a poynt of strong & a poynt of small Beer which me 3d. being in all 4½d. for supper. Here I paid 3d. for my bedd, and it was warmed with a warming pan, this being the first time I ever seed it done.

[*Page 14th*]   THURSDAY 13TH. JANY. 1774

Wind at E. so thick that I could not see above 100 yards distance. I crossed over Post down hill and Breackfast at Hamden, and after crossing a large barren Common of that name I dinned at Petersfield and then Got as far as Raik in the County of Sussex where I staid all night, having traveled twenty miles this which is more then I did expect carring my Box and Bundle on my back. They have for firing here, nothing but a kind heath like flaws.[10] At this pleace I paid 3d. for my bedd; My diet being all the old storry. Bread, Cheese & beer, and I hade a Rush Candle to light me to bedd.

FREIDAY 14TH.

This mor[n]ing I sold in my lodgings Sundry articles to the amount of 18/9 Str. which Articles cost me £1. 5. 6 Str. So that necessity obliged me to lose 6/9d. I then set foreward on the road and Breackfast at Libeck, and dinned at Roade Lane after crossing a Common 7 Miles long without a house upon it exceept one farm house near Libeck, and near the other end of the Common the road goes round a place called the Devils punch Bowl, and it may well be called so from it's Deepness and breathe and Shape of a Bowl. This night I lodged at Goodlaming in the County of Surry, having only traveled sixteen miles this day.

[*Page 15th*]   SATURDAY 15TH. JANY. 1774

This morning I breackfast at Gilford a pretty large toun. Then I passed Myra, and Hawsly places of no note and dinned at Effingham and then passed through Leatherhead and Eshted, at neither of the two last places I could get lodgings, and at the last place I hapned to fall in with two sailors in the same situation and we went foreward in the dark three Miles further to Epsom where we lodged & here I paid four pence for my Bedd, and four pence for my supper.

SUNDAY 16TH.

This day after breackfast and readg. some Chapters on a Newtestament I found in my room, I made the two following verses which I here insert below.

> My absent friends God bless, and those,
>   my wife and Childreen dear;

I pray for pardon to my foes,
And for them sheds a tear.
At Epsom here this day I ly,
Repenting my past sins;
Praying to Jesus for his mercy,
and success to my friends.

Here I hade an extream good dinner in Publick for sixpence. In the Afternoon I took a walk and seed round this place a great many fine Houses & gardens most of them belonging to Londoners.

[*Page 16th*]   MUNDAY 17TH. JAY. 1774

This day being verry rainy it was 10 AM before I set out, and before I got four Miles from Epsom I found my left Knee pain me much and before I got four miles farther which was to Wandsworth I would have given all the money I hade to have been at a Publick house for it quite fail'd me. Here I was glade to stay all night having only traveled Eight miles this day. This night I seed here a sawer of wood, who cou'd gain at that business Sixty Guinias a year if he woud keep close to his work; But he was in every respect the verry picture of Robie Smith in Lerwick and was in debt every where for Drink.

MUNDAY 18TH.

This day I got to London[11] and was like a blind man without a guide, not knowing where to go being freindless and having no more money but fifteen shillings & eight pence farthing a small sum to enter London with; But I trust in the mercys of God who is a rich provider and am hopefull before it is done some way will cast up for me. I took up my lodging at the old Ship Tavern in Little Hermitage Street,[12] Mr. George Newton being the landlord, but in Prison for debt at present.

[*Page 17th*]   WEDNESDAY 19 JAY. 1774

This day I shifted my cloaths and put on a clean Ruffled Shirt, clean Britches and waistcoat & my Brown Coat. I not having any other cloaths on ever since I left Lerwick but my blew Jacket and Bigg Coat above it & a plain shirt. At 11 AM I called to see Capt. Peery, but was told he would not be at home untill 5 pm. Having eat nothing for

24 houres, I dinned in my Lodging this day which cost me ½ Str. After dinner I took a walk with the mate of a ship a Scotsman who carried me through Virginia Street, London Street, part of White Chappel Street, down to London Hospitall, through Ragg fair, the Minnories Round Tour hill, and the Tour, through Saint Catharins, and Bur street and so home.[13]

At 5 pm called again at Capt. Perrys & the first face I saw was Willie Holcraw of Coningsburgh[14] who I found staid here as a servant, and while I was speacking to him, Capt. Perry came home & he immediatly knew me, and desired me to walk in which I did, and after sitting some time & drinking some tea, I called Capt. Perry aside and made my Intentions known to him, at same time begged his advice and assistance; He told me he hardly thought there would be any Business got for me in London. But told me to call on him at the Jamacia Coffee House[15] to morrow at Change time. I then went home, & soon went to Bedd.

[*Page 18th*]   THURSDAY 20TH JAY. 1774

This morning breackfast at home and paid 6d. for it. At noon called at the Jamacia Coffee House and soon after seed Capt. Perry & waited here and [at the?] Change untill 3 pm. but no appearance of any Business for me. The time I was in the Coffee house I drank 3ds. worth of punch, and I was obliged to make it serve me for Dinner. At night I hade ½d. worth of bread & 1d. of Cheese & a poynt of Porter for supper it being all I cou'd afford.

FREIDAY 21ST.

This morning I seed an advertisement for Bookeepers and Clerks to go to a Gentleman [at?] Philadelphia. I went as it directed to No. 1 in Catharine Court Princes street, but when I came there I was told they were served. I then waited again on Capt. Perry untill after 3 pm, But to no purpose. I this day offered to go steward of a ship bound to Maryland but could not get the birth. This day I was 3 or 4 miles through London and seed St. Pauls Church, the Bank of England where I seed the Gold lying in heaps, I also seed Summerst house, Gild hall, Drury Lane, Covingarden, Adelphus Buildings & severall other pleaces.[16] I then returnd and near my Lodgings I dinned at an eating house & hade 4d. worth of roast Beiff 1d. worth of bread & a poynt of small beer, in all 5½d.

This morning I seed an advertiesment in the Publick Ledger for a Messenger to a publick Lodge, Sallery 15/ Str. per week and another advertisement for an under Clerk to a Mercht. to both which I wrote answers and went to the places apointed, and found at each place more than a dozen of Letters before me, so that I hade litle expectation that way they being all weel acquanted and I a stranger. I then went to Change to see if any thing would cas[t] up but to no purpose, so I returned hom at 4 pm and spent the evening in a verry sollitary manner supping on bread & Cheese as usuall.

SUNDAY 23D.

This morning I drank some purle[17] for breackfast and then I took a walk in the forenoon through severall streets, and at 1 pm I returned to the eating house I hade formerly been at and dinned which cost me 6½ today having hade 1d. worth of pudding more than I formerly hade. In the afternoon I went to a Methodists Meeting, the Text was in the V Chap: Mathew and the 20th Verse. After sermon I came home and being solitarry in my room I made the following Verses which I insert on the other side of this leaf.

[*Page 20th*]   Now at London in a garret room I am,
          here frendless and forsaken;
          But from the Lord my help will come,
          Who trusts in him are not mistaken.

          When freinds on earth do faint and faile,
          And upon you their backs do turn;
          O Truely seek the Lord, and he will
          Them comfort that do murn.

          I'll unto God my prayer make,
          to him my case make known;
          And hopes he will for Jesus sake,
          Provide for me and soon.

MUNDAY 24TH.

This morning I wrote six tickets to give to shipmasters at Change seeking a stewards birth on board some ship, but could not get a birth.

I also wrote a petition in generall to any Mercht. or Tradesman setting forth my present situation, and the way in which I hade been brought up and where I hade served and in what station, at same time offering to serve any for the bare suport of life fore some time. But all to no effect, for all pleaces here at present are intierly carried by freinds and Intrest, And many Hundreds are sterving for want of employment, and many good people are begging.

[*Page 21st*]   TUESDAY 25TH. JANY. 1774

Having heard last night that John Ross sloop was come from Zetland, I took a Boat this morning and went on board her and seed him and Robert Irvine.[18] And then I hade the happiness to hear that my wife and Childrein were all well on the 3d. Inst. it being the day they left Bressaysound.[19] The rest of this day I was employed in presenting the Petition I hade draun up on the 24th. Inst. to severall Merchts. and others and doing all I cou'd to get into business of some kind near home but all to no effect.

WEDNESDAY 26TH.

This day I being reduced to the last shilling I hade was oblidged to engage to go to Virginia for four years as a schoolmaster[20] for Bedd, Board, washing and five pound during the whole time. I have also wrote my wife this day a particular Accot. of every thing that has happned to me since I left her untill this date; At 3 pm this day I went on board the Snow[21] Planter Capt. Bowers Comr. for Virginia now lying at Ratliff Cross, and imediatly as I came on board I recd. my Hammock and Bedding. At 4 pm came Alexr. Steuart on board the same Ship. He was Simbisters[22] Servt. and hade only left Zetland about three weeks before me. We were a good deall surprised to meet with on[e] another in this place.

[*Page 22d*]   THURSDAY 27TH. JAY. 1774

This day ranie weather. The ships crew imployed in rigging the ship under the Direction of the mate & I was imployed in getting my Hammock slung. At 2 pm came on board Alexr. Burnet nephew to Mr. Frances Farquharson writter in Edinburgh & one Samuel Mitchell a Cooper from Yorkshire[23] and both entred into the birth and Mace[24] with Stewart & me.

Freiday 28th.

This day the ships crew imployed as Yesterday.

Saturday 29th.

This day came on board Alexr. Kennedy[25] a young man from Edin-burgh who hade been a Master Cooper there and a Glasgow Man by trade a Barber[26] both which we took into our Mace, which com-pleated it being five Scotsmen and one Yorkshire man, and was always called the Scots Mace, And the Capt. told me he was from the Toun of Aberbothick in Scotland, but that he [had] note been there since he was fifteen years of age but hade been always in the Virginia trade which I was verry glade to hear.

Sunday 30th.

Hard frosty weather, keept onboard all day.

Munday 31st.

This day I went ashore and bought a penknife, a paper Book, and some paper and pens and came onboard to Dinner. It is surprising to see the No. of good tradesmen of all kinds, that come onboard every day.[27]

[*Page 23d.*]   Tuesday 1st. Feby. 1774

This morning the sails and provisions came on board. At noon it be-gun to snow verry hard & continoued snowing and freezing all night.

Wednesday 2d.

This day the ships crew imployed in bending the sails.

Thursday 3d.

This day more provisions came on board.

Freiday 4th.

This day at 7 AM unmoored from Ratliffcross and fell down the river with the tide there being no wind.

This day I seed Deptfoord, Greenage Hospitall, Blackwall and Ullage.[28] At 1 pm came to an anchor a little below the ½ way house. At 6 pm got under way again and fell down untill quite dark and then came to an Anchor a little above Pourfleet.

SATURDAY 5TH.

All this forenoon a verry thick fogg or rather hoar frost. At 2 pm it cleared up when one of the servants was turned ashore he being in a fiver and another so bad in it that he cou'd not be put ashore here.

SUNDAY 6TH.

At 7 AM got under way with a fair wind and clear wr. [weather] and at 11 AM came to an anchor off Gravesend and immediatly the Mercht. came on board and a Doctor & clerk with him and while the Clerk was fulling up the Indentures the doctor search'd every servt. to see that they were sound when two was turned ashore haveing the clap, and Seventy five were Intend[29] to Capt. Bowres for four Years.

[Page 24th]   MUNDAY 7TH. FEBY. 1774

This forenoon imployed in getting in provisions and water; at 4 pm put a servant ashore extreamly bade in a fiver, and then got under saile for Virginia with seventy Servants on board all indented to serve four years there at their differint Occoupations myself being one of the Number and Indented for a Clerk and Bookeeper, But when I aravied there I cou'd get no such birth as will appear in its place. At pm we came to an anchor at the Nore it blowing and snowing verry hard.

TUESDAY 8TH.

At 5 AM made saile from the Nore with the wind at W.N.W. Clear weather & blowing hard. At 2 pm got off a Pillot from Deall to take our River Pillot ashore for which Boat Capt. Bowers paid one and a half Guineas, and after buying some Gin here we stood streight to sea Under Close R. T. sails[30] and our fore saile, a verry high sea running all this day.

WEDNESDAY 9TH.

Wind at V.N.V. Steering V.B.S. in Company with the Price Freggate of Eighteen Guns bound to Jamacia. At noon caste out the Rs. [reefs?] out of the Topsailes.

Thursday 10th.

At 10 AM sighted the Isle of Wight. At three pm got a Pillot on board for Spithead at 15/. at 5 pm to an anchor there.

[*Page 25th*]   Freiday 11th. Feby. 1774

Wind at S.S.V. Blowing hard with heavy rain. At 10 AM dry and moderate weather. Shifted our mooring to the Mother bank closte along side of the Isle of Wight. In the Afternoon heavy Showrs of haile, & fresh gales all night.

Saturday 12th.

Wind as before, moderate weather and dry. In the afternoon was ½ Gill of Jeniver[31] [given?] every man on board.

Sunday 13th.

Wind at V.B.S. squally weather. Eight saile more at anchor in Company with us. At noon the Indented servants was like to mutiny against the Capt. for putting them to Allowance of bread & Mate, But it was soon quelled, Our Mace not Joyning with the rest. In the afternoon he went ashore, But before he left the Ship he called me and begged I wou'd stand by the Mate if there arose any disturbance among the rest of the servants.

Munday 14th.

Wind and weather as Yesterday; got a Quarter of fresh Beiff and some water on board.

Tuesday 15th.

Wind & weather as Yesterday.

Wednesday 16th.

Wind at N. At 4 pm came on a verry hard gale of wind. Struck

Topmasts and lowered Yards and got them fore and aft and paid out on the best Bower Cable.

[*Page 26th*]   THURSDAY 17TH. FEBY. 1774

Wind at N. The gale of wind still continous as yet. At 2 pm more moderate and then Capt. Bowers went ashore to buy more fresh provisions.

FREIDAY 18TH.

Wind as Yesterday. This day we was informed of a Ship being lost 11 Inst. on the back of the Isle of Wight. She was come from Virginia Load with Tobacco.

SATURDAY 19TH.

Wind at V.S.V. Blowing rainy weather. This day I sold my old Duffle coat to the Boatswan for 4/ Str.

SUNDAY 20TH.

Wind as Yesterday, fine moderate clear weather. This day I bought some bread, Cheese, suggar, & Gin to in all 1/5 Str.

MUNDAY 21ST.

Wind at N.N.V. Rainy blowing weather.

TUESDAY 22D.

Wind at S.B.V. This day I bought a penknife for six Biscuts having saved ten out of my allowance.

WEDNESDAY 23D.

Wind at V. such weather as yesterday.

THURSDAY 24TH.

Wind at V.N.V. Rany weather. At 5 pm came on an excessive hard gale of wind, was obliged to let go the small Bour Anchor, and Strich [strike?] Yards and Topmasts and get all the lower yards Lowered down and fore and aft.

[*Page 27th*]   FREIDAY 25TH. FEBY. 1774

Wind as yesterday; with squales & hard showrs of rain.

SATURDAY 26

Wind at N.B.E. fine moderate weather. Got up Yds. and Topmasts. At 10 AM The Capt. went ashore to get more fresh provisions, at 4 pm he came on board from Portsmouth with Bread, Beiff Pork and water and then imediatly got under saile and stood out to sea.

At this time we hade three men sick on board one with the flux, one with the fever and Ego,[32] and one frost bitt in his feet. At 11 pm the wind came all round to the N.V. Blowing verry hard. At Midnight close reefd the topsails.

SUNDAY 27TH.

Wind at N.V. At 4 AM Tack'd ship. At same time the man who was bade with the flux was found dead in his hammock. At 8 he was sewed up in it and at 9 AM he was burried in the sea after reading the service of the Dead over him, which was done by the Mate. At noon fine dry clear weather. One ship in sight. At 8 pm it began to Blow verry hard; close reeftd the topsails and at 11 pm stowd them.

MUNDAY 28TH.

Wind as Yesterday. At 4 AM wore ship under her courses, and then reefd the mainsaile and stood close by the wind for the Isle of Wight. At 9 AM sighted Feverie Point and then bore away for the Needles when we seed a large ship within the Breackers, but she happily got out again and went through the Needles with us they are three high Chalky rocks. Seed Hurst Castle, it is on a small sandy Island close to the Main, seed Yarmouth and Cowes both on the Isle of Wight. At 4 pm came to an Anchor on the Mother bank where we was before.

[*Page 28th*]   TUESDAY 1ST. MARCH 1774

Wind at N.V. dry weather. At 10 AM highesed a signall for the Pillot Boat. At 11 she came on board & carried what empty water cask we hade ashore. Last night and this morning was put in here by the gale of wind above 20 saile of ships.

This day I bought one Cotton napkin for three biscuits and a silk napkin for five Biscuits, both napkins half wore.

WEDNESDAY 2D.

Wind variable from V. to N. This day the Venerial disease was discovered upon one of the servants an Irish lad.

THURSDAY 3D.

Wind variable. This day a Blewbo[33] brock in the Groyne of the Irish lad and was dressed by a kind of a surgeon we hade. An Ugly sight it was to see.

FREIDAY 4TH.

Wind at V.S.V. fine moderate weather.

SATURDAY 5TH.

Wind at S.V.B.S. Bought one Loaf bread at 4d.

SUNDAY 6TH.

Wind and weather as Yesterday. Two servts. more taken ill.

MUNDAY 7TH.

Variable winds and rainy weather, nothing remarcable.

TUESDAY 8TH.

Wind at S.V. dry weather. Bought one pair trousers for seven Biscuits, a shoemakers hammer at four Do. and a musline stock with a pretty pinchback stocke Buckle for four pence and three biscuits. After 2 pm wind Variable with calms from S. to N.E.

[*Page 29th*]   WEDNESDAY 9 MARCH 1774

Wind at E.B.S. easy weather. Early this morning got under sail, and by noon left sight of the Isle of Wight under close reefd Topsails and our foresaile; blowing very hard with thick drissling rain and a high sea running from the westward all this day.

THURSDAY 10TH.

Wind and weather as yesterday, steering this day V.B.S. and V.S.V. The last 24 Hours the Snow went per logg 7½ Knots per Hour one hour with another. At noon left the Lands End of England. One Brigantine in Compy. with us bound for Jamacia.

FREIDAY 11TH.

Wind weather and course as yesterday. This forenoon clear but verry squally like. At 4 pm stowed the Main topsail and at 7 pm stowed fore Top-saile and close reefd the Main saile and scuded under it. The wind blowing excessive hard and a verry high sea running still from the westward. At 8 pm was obliged to batten down both fore and main hatches, and a little after I really think there was the odest shene betwixt decks that ever I heard or seed.

There was some sleeping, some spewing, some pishing, some shiting, some farting, some flyting, some daming, some Blasting their leggs and thighs, some their Liver, lungs, lights and eyes, And for to make the shene the odder, some curs'd Father Mother, Sister, and Brother.

SATURDAY 12TH.

Wind weather and course as before. We are now past the skirts of the Bay of Biscay and entred into the Atlantick Ocean, going at the rate of 8 knots per houre.

[*Page 30th*]   SUNDAY 13TH. MARCH 1774

Wind at S.S.E. cour[s]e V.B.S. At 11 AM Moderate weather. Let out all reefs. At noon in Latitude 44 North per observation. This after-noon got most of sick and ailing to deck the number of which I really cannot now ascertain. But I thank God I have as yet kept my health weel. At 3 pm there was two servants put in Irons for wanting other than what was served. But they were soon released on there asking pardon and promising to behave better.

MUNDAY 14TH.

Wind and weather as yesterday. Steering S.V.B.V. At 10 AM got up the main Topgallon mast and the Yard aCross and set the Main Topgallon saile and stouten [studding?] sailes below and aloft. This day we was served salt Codd, Oile & winegar for Dinner.

TUESDAY 15TH.

Wind at N.N.V. steering S.V. fine warm sun shine wr. At 8 pm came on in an instant an excessive hard gale of wind with rain and we were imediatly oblidged to bring the ship under reef'd courses.

WEDNESDAY 16TH.

Still blowing fresh and a high Sea running the Vessel yet und[er] her Courses.

THURSDAY 17TH.

Moderate weather. At 7 AM sett the close reefd Topsails. At noon in Lat. 38:1 North. At 8 pm was oblidged to hand the Topsails and

take a reef in the Mainsaile, and at 9 pm sett the reefd Topsails again, the weather being verry unconstant.

[*Page 31st*]   FREIDAY 18TH. MARCH 1774

Wind at N.N.V. steering V.S.V. At noon in Lat 37.10 N. Fine clear warm weather.

SATURDAY 19TH.

Wind at V. steering S.S.V. moderate weather. At noon put about ship and steered N.B.V. At noon in Latitude 36 North going about 3½ Knots per logg.

SUNDAY 20TH.

Wind at N.N.V. fine weather, steering V.S.V. At 10 AM seed a Vessell steering S. about 4 Leagues distance. At noon in Lat. 34:35 North.

MUNDAY 21ST.

Quite calm all day. At 8 AM put out the Jolly Boat and catched three small Tortoise about 18 Inches long and 14 Inches Broad.

TUESDAY 22D.

Wind as before, steering S.V. This day we seed two large Chirks[34] pass by the Vessell and the Pillot fish along with them. At noon in Lat 31:24 North. At 8 pm sprung up a fresh breise at N.N.E. then steered V.S.V. At 10 going 8 Knots per logg.

WEDNESDY. 23D.

Wind as yesterday blowing fresh, steering V.S.V. and a verry high sea running all this day.

THURSDY. 24TH.

Wind, weather & Course as yesterday, going 8 knots per logg.

FREIDAY 25TH.

Wind and weather as before going per logg 7½ knots. At noon in Lat. 29:18 North. Then the Capt. ordered the man at the helm to steer V. ½ South.

[*Page 32d*]   ### SATURDAY 26 MARCH 1774

Wind at E.N.E. steering V. per Compass. At 4 AM got into the trade wind, at noon in Lat. 27:59 North.

SUNDAY 27TH.

Wind, weather, and course, as yesterday. At 8 AM got up all hammocks and the sick likways they being now in number about 37, there being th[ree] sick in our mace Vizt. Stewart, Burnet, and the Yorkshire Cooper. At noon we all betwixt decks cleand out, and washed with wineggar.

MUNDAY 28TH.

Wind at E.B.N. Steering V.B.N. At noon in Lat 26:18 North, fine warm weather. At 4 pm Rigged and set the main Topgallonroyal, going per logg 4 knots.

TUESDAY 29TH.

Wind, weather, and course as yesterday. Going 5 knots with Royals, Stoutensails and Driver all sett. At noon in Lat. 26:38 north.

WEDNESDAY 30TH.

Fine warm weather, wind & course as before.

THURSDAY 31ST.

Wind, weather, and cours as before. The sick are now increased to the number of fifty betwixt decks, besides three in the steerage Vizt. two seamen and a passanger. There is now a deall of sea weed passing us every day from the Gulf of Florida.

FREIDAY 1 APLL. 1774

Wind, weather and course as before. At 5 AM catched a flying fish, it is much of the sise & couler of a May puttuck[35] but not so thick over the shoulders, and it has a fin at each shoulder that reaches to it's taile by which it flies as long as they are out.

[Page 33d]   SATURDAY 2D. APLL. 1774

The wind, weather, and course are still the same as last. Since this day [a?] week that we got into the trade winds we have gone betwixt 4 & 6 knots every houre per logg. At 2 pm died one of the servts. in a fever & palsie and was burried the same night, the Mate reading the service of the dead over him as before.

SUNDAY 3D.

Wind weather and course as before. Last night Alexr. Stewart was so high in the fever that I sat up with him all night, and Burnet & the Cooper are still verry bad, but not so high as Stewart. This day the Capt. ordred some Cock & hen to be killed and fresh broth made for the sick.

Munday 4th.

Wind weather & course still as before and Jogging on from 4 to 6 knots at an average per houre. At 5 pm I was oblidged to get Stewart blister'd and satt up again all night with him, having become his nurse for Country sake he being the first in the Mace that was taken ill, and I was not sure how soon it might be my own fate. But thank God I am as yet well and hearty. This night I supped on a dish called Scratch-platters. It is made of biscuits broack small and soacked in water untill they are soft, and then Winegar, oile, salt, and Onions cut small put to it, and supped with spoons.

Tuesday 5th.

Wind at E.S.E., fine warm weather, course V.B.N. At noon in Lat. 27:17 North going per logg as before.

[Page 34th]   ### Wednesday 6th Apll. 1774

Wind weather and course as yesterday. There is still a great number of Sick on board mostly of the fever. At 4 pm wind at S.S.W. we being now out of the trade winds, and in Lat. 27:37 North. At 5 pm hauled down Stouten sails, Main Topgallon saile & in Driver. At 6 pm came on a verry hard squale of wind with heavy rain which continoued untill midnight.

I have wore no Britches nor stockins since we got into the trade winds, only a pair of long trousers down to my buckles. And this day having put on a shorter pair untill my longest pair was wash'd, I got both my Ancles burned by the sun, it so verry hot here.

Thursday 7th.

Variable winds and Calms. At 6 AM seed a large ship to windwar'd, and she imediatly highsed her colours and bore doun upon us. She proved to be the York off and from Bristoll Will: Rose Mr. Bound for York River in Virginia.[36]

Freiday 8th.

Wind at E.S.E. fine weather. The York still in Compy. with us. At 8 AM seed a Vessel to windward of us standing W. homeward bound as we imagind. At noon in Lat. 28:14 North. This day the Chief Mate imployed in Painting the ship from the Gunell doun to the Bright Sides all round head & stern likeways. At 3 pm spack with the York again.

[Page 35th]   Saturday 9th. Apll. 1774

Wind at E.S.E. steering per Compass W.N.W. fine dry warm weather. At 6 AM sett Topgallon and T. G. Royall, with Stouten sails below and aloft and the drivers, in head of the York about 8 Miles. At 8 pm a great deall of Thunder and lightning and at 10 pm it began to blow fresh going at the rate of 8 knots & odds.

Sunday 10th.

Wind at S.W. steering N.W. At 6 AM the York so far astern that we coud only see her from the deck, we then shortned saile for her. At 8 AM came on verry heavy rains with squals of wind and then calms. At noon in Latitude 29:30. We are now neare Barbadoes where it is always unconstant weather Viz. Thunder, lightning, gales of wind, heavy rains and Calms. At 2 pm the York about 3 Miles astern, at same time seed another ship in head of us standing south.

Munday 11th.

Wind at N. steering W.N.W. At 8 AM spack with the York. At noon in Lat: 30:19. North.

Tuesday 12th.

Wind at N.W. steering W.S.W. At 5 AM seed a small vessell to windward [and] at 8 lay too in order to speack with her as did the York. At 9 AM spack with her, she proved to be a schooner from North Carolina load with Boards, Bound for Dominico. She hade been 9 days out and was in Long 63½ W on the 2d. Inst. [when] they hade a verry hard gale of wind which wracked and drove ashore a great many ships at North Carolina. At same time spake with the York who hade got a verry fine Dolpine this mor[n]ing, and he sent the ½ of it on board to Capt. Bowers with a line. At noon in Lat. 30. North, at 6 pm came on a hard gale of wind, close reef'd both T. sails.

[*Page 36th*]   Wednesday 13th. Apll. 1774

Wind, and weather as yesterday the gale still continouing. At 8 AM stowd the fore T. saile, at noon stowd the Main T. Saile. The York doing the same. In Lat: 29:11 North. At 2 pm seed a small sloop standing S.S.W. At 4 pm stowd the fore saile and Brought the ship too under a Close reef'd Main saile, the gale continouing.

Thursday 14th.

Still lying too, the York doing the same und[er] bare pouls. This forenoon the ships Crew imployed in setting up the Rigging. At 6 pm sett Close reefd Topsails and spake with the York, who had catched two large Dolphines. She sent one of them on bord us by a line as before: it was the prettiest fish I ever saw, and when they are alave in the water it changes itself into all coulers. But I think he keeps mostly by a saxon blew. The York then sett her close reef'd Topsailes.

Freiday 15th.

Wind at N.N.W. moderate weather. At 5 AM let out all reefs, steering close by the wind Viz W. At same time spake with the York and they agreed to s[t]eer N.W. if the wind wou'd allow them. At noon in Lat. 28:18 North. This day our Cheiff Mate Mr. James Jones was taken verry bade of the fever.

SATURDAY 16TH.

Wind at V.S.W. steering N.W. At 5 AM the York in head of us as far as we cou'd see her. Made all the saile we could and at 10 AM came up and spake with her she lying too for us. Mr. Jones fever increases. At 11 AM he sent for me & begged me to sett his head and attend him during his illness as he cou'd not indure the Doctor to touch him. At 4 pm spak with the York again, & he sent on board 4 bottles Rum & every man hade a dram.

[*Page 37th*]   SUNDAY 17TH. APLL. 1774

Wind at S.W. light Breeses, at noon in Lat. 29:34. North. All this day Capt. Bowrs verry uneasy and Mr. Jones verry high in the fever, and Stewart has relapsed again into it, since I came to wait on Mr. Jones.

MUNDAY 18TH.

Wind as yesterday. Steering N.W.B.N., at noon in Lat. 29:53. The York still in Company. Capt. Bowres something easier to day, but Mr. Jones continous as yesterday. At 6 pm Mr. Jones hade a blister put to his back.

TUESDAY 19TH.

Wind weather and course as yesterday. This forenoon Mr. Jones easier and quite sencible after the blistering. At noon in Lat. 30:44 North. At 4 pm the York as far a stern as we cou'd see her which oblidged us to ly too for her. At 10 pm she came up and spack with us & they again agreed on the course to be steered. This day I brought up Mr. Jones Journall for five days back, also Capt. Bowrs Journall for four days back and at same time begged me to mark the Logg Book and ordred that whoever hade the charge of watch to aquant me what the ship went per Logg &ca.

WEDNESDAY 20TH.

Wind, weather and course as before, the York in Compy. Stewart now begins to mend again and this day I assisted Mr. Jones in getting up to deck, but he is still excessive weak. The fever and ague now begins to rage among the servants & sailors.

[*Page 38th*]   THURSDAY 21ST. APLL. 1774

This morning a young lad, one of the servts. being verry ill with the Fever and Ague, he begged me to apply to Mr. Jones the Chief Mate, and told me he cou'd give him something that would cure him; Mr. Jones first desired me to give him a womite and then wrote the following lines on a slip of paper and after folding it up gave it to me, to see it tyed up in the corner of his handkirchif or Cravat and vear it at his breast next his skin with strick charge to him not to look at it himself nor let any other person see it or look at it untill he was got wel. The words are as follows.

> When Jesus saw the Cross he trembled,
> The Jews said unto him why tremblest thou,
> You have neither got an Ague nor a fever.
> Jesus answered and said unto them
> I have neither got an Ague nor a fever
> But whosoever keepeth my words
> Shall neither have an Ague nor a fever.

Mr. Jones told me when he gave me the above coppy it [was] a sertain cure for the fever and Ague, the paitient being first womited and then wearing the lines as above directed, But if they show it to any or look at it themselves it will have no effect.

FREIDAY 22D.

This day I was seased with a sever Cold and Aching in my bones, But I thank God I am weel car'd for & has every thing sent me from the Cabin I can desire.

[*Page 39th*]   SATURAY 23D. APLL. 1774

Wind at S.W. Light Airs of it, steering N.W.B.N. I am this day horse in my throat, But stiring about.

SUNDAY 24TH.

Wind &ca. as yesterday. I am confined to my hammock.

Munday 25th.

Wind &ca. as before, And I am still confined with the Aching in my bones.

Tuesday 26th.

Wind &ca. as before, I having got a sweat am greatly better.

Wednesday 27th.

This morning I am fairly got the better of my cold and the Aching in my bones and am able to stir about.

It being quite thick all last night and this morning we have lost sight of the York. At 11 AM it Cleared up and fine weather. At noon struck soundings in 35 fm. water Reed sand, sounded again at 4 pm and hade 18 Fm. white sand, sounded at 6 pm & hade 13 Fm. white sand & shells. Every man now looking out for land or rather for trees first. At 7 pm we made Cape Henry and the Coast plain. We then highesed our flagg for a Pillot Boat and at   pm we hade four Pillot boats along side, and Capt. Bowrs took one Mr. Cooper who brought us within the Capes, and to an Anchor at 10 pm where we lay all night.

Thursday 28th.

At 7 AM the Pillot wegh'd Anchor and wrought the ship up to Hampton Roads where we came to an Anchor at 10 AM. This morning I was employed in Making out a Clean list of the servants names and [*Page 40th*] Business and age, and how soon I was done Capt. Bowers went ashore in the Pillot boat to Hamton on Elizabeth river. We have some goods to put out before we leave this place. At night, a deall of Thunder, lightning and rain.

Freiday 29th.

Wind at N.N.W. verry rainy weather untill 9 AM. At 11 AM there came a boat on board from Hampton for goods which she received; latter part of the day fresh gales.

Saturday 30th.

Wind at N.W. Blowing hard all day, at Anchor in Hampton Roads.

Sunday 1st. May 1774

Wind, weather and at Anchor as yesterday.

Munday 2d.

Wind as before, fine fair warm weather. Got out the rest of the goods that was for Hampton. At 2 pm the Capt. Carried five servts. ashore to Hampton in order to sell their Indentures, But returned again at Mid-night with[out?] selling any more but one Boat Builder.[37] He brought on board with him four Barrells Virginia Pork and one Puncheon Do. rum, & 3 live hogs.

Tuesday 3d.

Wind at W.N.W. fine moderate weather. At 6 AM weigh'd Anchor from Hampton Roads, and stood out to Sea untill we made the Entry of Rappahannock river, which we did at 10 AM, proceeding up the same for Fredericksburgh. At 6 pm came to an Anchor at Arrabanna.[38]

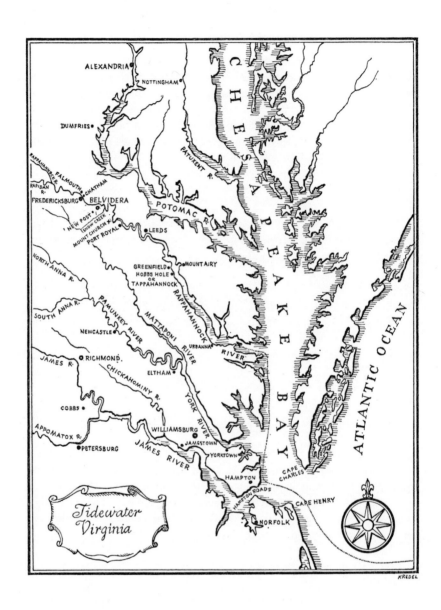

ALEXANDRIA

NOTTINGHAM

DUMFRIES

PATUXENT R.

RAPPAHANNOCK FALMOUTH

RAPIDAN R.

CHATHAM

FREDERICKSBURG BELVIDERA

POTOMAC R.

NEW POST

SNOW CREEK

MOUNT CHURCH

PORT ROYAL

LEEDS

NORTH ANNA R.

GREENFIELD

HOBBS HOLE

OR

TAPPAHANNOCK

MOUNT AIRY

SOUTH ANNA R.

PAMUNKEY RIVER

MATTAPONI RIVER

RAPPAHANNOCK

RIVER

NEWCASTLE

URBANNA

RICHMOND

JAMES R.

CHICKAHOMINY R.

ELTHAM

YORK RIVER

COBBS

APPOMATOX R.

WILLIAMSBURG

PETERSBURG

JAMES RIVER

JAMESTOWN

YORKTOWN

HAMPTON

CAPE
CHARLES

HAMPTON ROADS

CAPE HENRY

NORFOLK

CHESAPEAKE BAY

ATLANTIC OCEAN

Tidewater
Virginia

KREDEL

36

[*Page 41st*]   WEDNESDAY 4TH MAY 1774

Wind at N.N.W. excessive cold all this forenoon. At 2 pm weigh'd and in order to work up the river with the tide, But cou'd gain nothing the wind being against us.

THURSDAY 5TH.

Wind as Yesterday hard frost this morning, forenoon warm and calm with sunshine. At noon wegh'd Anchor & stood up the river untill dark, and then came to an Anchor 6 or 8 Miles above the Town of Arrabanna.

FREIDAY 6TH.

Wind as before. At 4 AM got under saile & stood up the river and at 9 AM passed by the Town of Hobshole[39] and let it on our Larboard hand as we did the Town of Arrabanna. At Hobshole there was five Glasgow ships and an English Brigantine lying. At 2 pm we passed by Leedstown[40] on our Starboard hand where there was a ship from London lying with Convicts. At night came to Anchor about 6 Miles above Leedstown.

SATURDY 7TH.

This morning thick weather. At 10 AM got under way and stood up to Port Royall[41] on our Larboard hand where we aravied at 2 pm, The Capt. going ashore to change his Pillot, and at 4 pm returned with Another and we imediatly got under way again and got about 7 miles above Port Royall before dark. All along both sides of the River there is nothing to be seen but woods in the blossom, Gentlemens seats & Planters houses.

[*Page 42d*]   SUNDAY 8 MAY 1774

Early this morning died the old German, a man between 60 & 70 years of Age. At 5 AM weigh'd Anchor and tow'd & warped up, it being quite calm. At 9 AM was obliged to come to an Anchor, and ly untill the tide made, and then wegh'd and got about 3 Miles above Port Morton[42] where we lay all night. This forenoon we lost one of our live hogs, he Ju[m]ping overboard & swiming ashore and imediatly got into the woods. At night the Capt. carried the old German ashore and Burried him somewhere in the woods.

MUNDAY 9TH.

At 4 AM weighd and towd and warped up all day. Light airs of wind right in head.

TUESDAY 10TH.

At 2 AM wegh'd and stood up with the tide, came to an Anchor at 6 AM & lay untill Do. 8 when we weigh'd with a fair wind & got to our Moorings at 6 pm at the Toun of Fredericksburgh.[43]

WEDNESDAY 11TH.

At 10 AM Both Coopers & the Barber from our Mace went ashore upon tryall. At night one Daniel Turner[44] a servt. returned on board from Liberty so drunk that he abused the Capt. Cheif Mate & Boatswan to a verry high degree, which made to be horse whipt. put in Irons and thumb screwed. An houre after he was unthumbscrewed, taken out of the Irons, but then he was hand cuffed, and gagged all night.

[*Page 43d*]   THURSDAY 12TH MAY 1774

All hands quite on board this day. Turner ungagged But continoued in handcuffs.

FREIDAY 13TH.

This forenoon put ashore here what bale goods we hade remaining on board. In the afternoon Mr. Burnet, Stewart and myself went ashore on liberty to take a walk and see the Toun, who's principall street is about half an English Mile long, the houses generally at a little distance one from another, some of them being built of wood & some of them of brick, and all covered with wood made in the form of slates about four Inches broad, which when painted blew you wou'd not know it from a house sclated with Isedell sclate.[45] In this Toun the Church, the Counsell house, the Tolbooth the Gallows & the Pillary are all within 130 yds. of each other. The Market house is a large brick building a litle way from the Church.[46] Here we drank some Bottles of beer of their own brewing and some bottles of Cyder for which we paid 3½ per bottle of each. Returned on board in the evening. Turner still in handcuffs.

SATURDAY 14TH.

Nothing remarcable. Turner still in handcuffs.

SUNDAY 15TH.

All last night a great deall of thunder & Lightning. This day Mr. Anderson[47] came to toun and came on bord, and spacke to severall of the servts. Turner still handcuff'd.

[*Page 44*]   MUNDAY 16TH MAY 1774

This day severalls came on board to purchase servts. Indentures and among them there was two Soul drivers. They are men who make it their bussines to go on board all ships who have in either Servants or Convicts and buy sometimes the whole and sometimes a parcell of them as they can agree, and then they drive them through the Country like a parcell of Sheep untill they can sell them to advantage, but all went away without buying any.[48]

TUESDAY 17TH.

This day Mr. Anderson the Mercht. sent for me into the [cabin?] and verry genteely told me that on my recomendations he would do his outmost to get me settled as a Clerk or bookeeper if not as a schoolmaster which last he told me he thought wou'd turn out more to my advantage upon being settled in a good famely.

The ships crew and servants imployed in getting ashore all the cask out of the hould, no sales this day.

WEDNESDAY 18TH.

This day the ships crew and servants imployed in getting out the ballast and unrigging the ship. One Cooper, one Blacksmith & one Shoemaker were settled with Masters this day.

THURSDAY 19TH.

One Farmer's time sold & one Cabinet Maker on tryall.

FREIDAY 20TH.

This day we got the first four Hhds. of Tobacco on board; Turner still continous handcuffed.

[*Page 45*]   SATURDAY 21ST MAY 1774

This day one Mr. Cowly a Man twixt fifty & sixty years of age, a servt., also three sons of his their ages from Eight to fourteen were all settled with one McDonald a Scotsman.[49]

SUNDAY 22D.

All hands quiet on board.

MUNDAY 23D.

This morning a great number of Gentlemen and Ladies driving into Town it being an anuall Fair day[50] & tomorrow the day of the Horse races. At 11 AM Mr. Anderson begged [me] to settle as a schoolmaster with a freind of his one Colonel Daingerfield and told me he was to be in Town tomorrow, or perhaps to night, and how soon he came he shou'd aquant me. At same time all the rest of the servants were ordred ashore to a tent at Fredericksbg. and severall of their Indentures were then sold. About 4 pm I was brought to Colonel Daingerfield, when we imediatly agreed and my Indenture for four years was then delivered him and he was to send for me the next day. At same time ordred to get all my dirty Cloaths of every kind, washed at his expence in Toun; at night he sent me five shillings on board by Capt. Bowers to keep my pocket.

TUESDAY 24TH. MAY 1774

This morning I left the Ship at 6 AM having [*Page 46th*] been sixteen weeks and six days on board her. I hade for Breackfast after I came ashore one Chappin[51] sweet milk for which I paid 3½ Cury. At 11 AM went to see a horse race about a mille from Toun, where there was a number of Genteel Company as well as others. Here I met with the Colonel again and after some talk with him he gave me cash to pay for washing all my Cloaths and Something over. The reace was gain'd by a Bay Mare, a white boy ridder. There was a gray Mare started with the Bay a black boy ridder but was far distant the last heat.[52]

WEDNESDAY 25TH.

I Lodged in a Tavern last night and paid 7½ for my Bedd and 7½ for my breackfast. This morning a verry heavy rain untill 11 AM. Then I recd. my Linens &ca. all clean washed and packing every thing up I went on board the ship and Bought this Book for which I paid 18d. Str. I also bought a small Divinity book called the Christian Monitor[53] and a spelling book, both at 7½ & an Arithmetick at 1/6d. all for my own Accot.

THURSDAY 26TH.

This day at noon the Colonel sent a Black with a cuple of Horses for me and soon after I set out on Horseback and aravied at his seat of Belvidera about 3 pm and after I hade dined the Colonel took me to a neat little house at the upper end of an Avenue of planting at 500 yds. from the Main house, where I was [*Page 47th*] to keep the school, and Lodge myself in it.

This pleace is verry pleasantly situated on the Banks of the River Rappahannock about seven Miles below the Toun of Fredericksburgh, and the school's right above the Warff so that I can stand in the door and pitch a stone on board of any ship or Boat going up or coming doun the river.

FREIDAY 27TH.

This morning about 8 AM the Colonel delivered his three sons to my Charge to teach them to read write and figure. His oldest son Edwin 10 years of age, intred into two syllables in the spelling book, Bathourest his second son 6 years of age in the Alphabete and William his third son 4 years of age does not know the letters. He has likeways a Daughter whose name is Hanna Basset Years of age.[54] Soon after we were all sent for to breackfast to which we hade tea Bread, Butter & cold meat and there was at table the Colonel, his Lady, his Childreen, the housekeeper and myself. At 11 AM the Colonel and his Lady went some where to pay a visite, he upon horseback and she in her Charriot. At 2 pm I dined with the Housekeeper the Childreen and a Stranger Lady. At 6 pm I left school, and then I eat plenty of fine straw berries, but they neither drink Tea in the afternoon nor eat any supper here for the most part. My school Houres is from 6 to 8 in the Morning, in the forenoon from 9 to 12 and from 3 to 6 in the afternoon.

[*Page 48th*]   SATURDAY 28TH. MAY 1774

Nothing remarcable this day. In the evening the Colonel and his Lady returned from their visite.

SUNDAY 29TH.

There is no Church nearer Belvidera than Fredericksburgh, and for want of a sadle I was oblidged to stay at home all day and when I was alone in the school I the[n] thought on the following verses.

1st.

In Virginia now I am, at Belvidera settled,
    but may they ever mercy find, who hade the cause
that I am from my sweet wife seperated
    And Oblidged to leave my Infant Children, Fatherless.

2d.

As a schoolmaster, I am here;
    And must for four years, remain so;
May I indeavour the Lord to fear,
    and always his commands do.

3d.

For in Gods strength I do rely,
    that he at his appointed time,
Will bring me back to my family,
    if I his precepts do but mind.

4th.

O May my God provide for them,
    Who unto me are near and dear;
tho they afar off me are from,
    O Jesus keep them in thy fear.

[Page 49th]   ### 5th.

Do thou enable me to labour,
    and my fortune do thou mend;
that what I get by thy favour,
    I to my family may send.

6th.

O Lord my God do thou them save
    from dangers and from death
and may they food and rayment have
    and for the same may thankfull be while they have breath.

7th.

And may we all ever gloryfie thy name
    and loud thy praises sing
and unto all make known the fame
    of Jehova our almighty King.

8th.

O ever blessed be the Lord,
    the King of all the earth is he,
let us exalt his name with one Accord
    and thankfull unto him be ye.

                                        Finis.

After dinner I took a walk about a Miles distance from the house along the high way, and by the road side seed a Corn Mill, and another pretty house called Snow Creek[55] belonging to the Colonel.

[*Page 50th*]   MUNDAY 30TH. MAY 1774

Nothing remarcable this day.

TUESDAY 31ST.

This day there was about fifty white Ewe's and lambs feeding twix the main house and the school door and so tame that they wou'd come and look in at the door & see what we was doing. The lambs here are as large here at this date as in Zetland at Michelsmass; being of the english bread.

WEDNESDAY 1ST. JUNE 1774

This day there was prayers in all the Churches in Virginia on Accot. of the disagreement at present betwixt great Brittain and her Colonies in North America, on Accot. of their not agreeing to pay a duty on Tea laid on them by the british parliment and the Bostonians destroying a Quantity of Tea belonging to the British East India Compy. in 1773.[56]

THURSDAY 2D.

This day nothing remarcable.

FREIDAY 3D.

This day I eat green pease at dinner this being the the last of them this season here.

SATURDAY 4TH.

Nothing remarcable.

SUNDAY 5TH.

Do. at home all day.

MUNDAY 6TH.

Do. remarcable.

TUESDAY 7TH.

Do. remarcable.

[*Page 51st*]　　　WEDNESDAY 8TH JUNE 1774

This day I eat plenty of fine ripe Cherries brought out of the woods this morning by the Colonel.

THURSDAY 9TH.

Nothing remarcable.

FREIDAY 10TH.

Recd. two pair fine new brown thread stockins.

Below is an Inventory of the Cloaths &ca. I brought to Belvidera with me Vizt.

One Superfine Brown Cloath Coat full mounted
One Do. vest Coat.
One floored [flowered] Silk Do.
One fine marsyled [marseilles] Do.
One Brown Duffel Do.
One pair new Black Stockins Britches
One pair new Doe Skin—Do.
One pair flannen Drawers
One pair Osenburgh [Osnaburg] Do.
Six Ruffled Shirts
five plain white Do.
One Cheque—Do.
One Blew Cloath Jacket
Seven Musline Stocks
One Black silk Cravate
One pair Ribbed Cotton Stockins
Ten pair, worsted Do.
One new Hatt and one Do. Wigg
five pocket Napkins.
two hand Towels.
two pair Trousers

One pair Shoes; with Pinchback shoe, stock & knee buckles
One Trunk, with fine lock and hinges.
Severall other Articles besides what are here mentioned but are
too tedeous to mention.

[*Page 52d*]   SATURDAY 11TH. JUNE 1774

At 9 AM left the school and went a fishing on the River with the
Colonel his eldest [son] and another Gentleman in two Canoes. Mrs.
Dangerfield another Lady and the other two Boys mett us at Snow
Creek in the Chair at 2 pm when we all dined on fish under a tree.

SUNDAY 12TH.

This day at Church in Fredericksburgh and at same time settled a
Correspondance at Glasgow for getting letters from home, by their
being put under cover to Messrs. Anderson & Horsburgh Merchts.
in Do. and the expence charged to Mr. Glassel Mercht. in Fredericksbg. Virginia.[57]

MUNDAY 13TH.

Nothing remarcable.

TUESDAY 14TH.

This morning entred to school Willm. Pattie son to John Pattie
wright,[58] and Salley Evens daughter to Thomas Evens Planter.[59] This
day I wrote my wife a particular Accot. of all my transactions since I
wrote her from London 26th. Jany. last, the Coppy of which I have
by me.

WEDNESDAY 15TH.

Nothing remarcable.

THURSDAY 16TH.

This eveng the Colonel told me he hade about 400 Acres of land in
wheat and as much in Indian Corn every year and that he comonly
exported about 3600 bushels of wheat every Year besides serving his
own Family. But that he did not expect to have above the one half

this year owing to a strong frost they hade in Aprile last. Wheate at 5/ per Bushel.

[*Page 53d*]   FREIDAY 7TH. JUNE 1774

This day recd. two pair new Rushia drill britches and two new short Coats of Brown Holland.

SATURDAY 18TH.

Nothing remarcable.

SUNDAY 19TH.

At home all day.

MUNDAY 20TH.

This morning entred to school Philip & Dorothea Edge's Children of Mr. Benjamin Edge Planter.[60]

Same day Colonel Daingerfield began to cut down his wheat, which they do with a syth.[61]

TUESDAY 21ST.

This day Mr. Samuel Edge Planter came to me and begged me to take a son of his to scholl who was both deaff and dum, and I consented to try what I cou'd do with him.

WEDNESDAY 22D.

Nothing remarcable.

THURSDAY 23D.

This day entred to school John Edge son to the above named Mr. Sam: Edge. He is a lad about 14 years of age and is both deaff and Dum.[62]

FREIDAY 24TH.

Nothing remarcable.

SATURDAY 25TH.

This afternoon I went and took a walk in the wheat field and under a tree I filled all my pockets of as fine walnuts as ever I eat, But so hard a shell that I was oblidged to have a hammer to breack them.

[*Page 54th*]   SUNDAY 26 JUNE 1774

After Breackfast I took a walk 3 Miles to Mr. Edge's, the dum lad's fathers where I dined and drank some grogg and returned home in the afternoon. At night I hade a small Congregation of Negroes, lear[n]ing their Catechisim and hearing me read to them.

MUNDAY 27TH.

Nothing remarcable.

TUESDAY 28TH.

Do. . . Do.

WEDNESDAY 29TH.

Do. . . Do.

THURSDAY 30TH.

Do. . . Do.

FREIDAY 1ST JULY 1774.

Do. . . Do.

SATURDAY 2D.

Do. . . Do.

SUNDAY 3D.

At home all the forenoon. In the afternoon went to see one Mr. Richards[63] an Overseer and his wife where I eat plenty of honney out of the Comb, it being taken out of a Beehive in a tree in the woods last night.

MUNDAY 4TH.

Nothing remarcable.

TUESDAY 5TH.

Do. . . Do.

WEDNESDAY 6TH.

Do. . . Do.

THURSDAY 7TH.

Do. . . Do.

[*Page 55th*]   FREIDAY 8TH. JULY 1774

After school houres I went two Miles to see the Taylor who made my Cloaths he being a Brittoner but married to a Buckskine, and I found his wife and Daughters drinking tea, at which I Joyned them, The Taylor not being at home.[64]

SATURDAY 9TH.

Nothing remarcable.

SUNDAY 10TH.

At home all day.

MUNDAY 11TH.

Nothing remarcable.

TUESDAY 12TH.

Sold the spelling book that I bought on board the Planter 25th. May last, and got the same money for it that I paid for the Christian Monitor and it.

WEDNESDAY 13TH.

Nothing remarcable.

Thursday 14th.

This day at noon Colonel Daingerfield's wheat field was set on fire, by one of the Stackers letting the fire fall from his pipe, and above twenty Bushels wheat burned before the fire could be stopt, notwithstanding there was ods of forty white and black about it—white & black people.

[*Page 56th*]   Freiday 15th. July 1774.

Nothing remarcable.

Saturday 16th.

This afternoon the Colonel finished the cutting down of His wheat which cost of wages to hired people £23. 10 Curcy, besides their wictualls and drink.

Sunday 17th.

At home all day.

Munday 18th.

This morning entred to School Lewis Richards.[65] Same day I put on a pair of new shoes made in Fredericksburgh of English calf leather the price of them 12/6 Curcy. Same day gave one pair of old worsted Stockins for 22 foot of Gum plank 10 Inch broad and one thick to make me a Chest.

Tuesday 19th.

On Freiday 15th. Inst. John Edge the Dumb lad left the school at 6 pm and has not returned since.

Wednesday 20th.

On Munday 4th. Inst. at 6 pm William Pattie left the school and has not returned since.

Thursday 21st.

Nothing remarcable.

Freiday 22d.

Do. remarcable.

Saturday 23d.

Do. remarcable.

Sunday 24th.

Went to Church on Horseback along with the Colonel, Text 28th. Chaptr. & 28th. Verse of the Book of Job.

[*Page 57th*]   Munday 25th. July 1774

Nothing remarcable. Jno. Edge returd. to school.

Tuesday 26th.

Nothing remarcable.

Wednesday 27th.

Do. . . . Do.

Thursday 28th.

Do. . . . Do.

Freiday 29th.

Do. . . . Do.

Saturday 30th.

Do. . . . Do.

Sunday 31st.

This morning at 4 AM Mrs. Daingerfield was delivered of a Son; Myself at home all day.

Munday 1st. August 1774

Nothing remarcable.

Tuesday 2d.

Do. . . Do.

Wednesday 3d.

Philip & Dorathea Edge's left the School on Freiday 22d. of last Month at 6 pm and has not returned since. Last night after I hade put out the Candle and gone to bedd I was obliged to get up again & put on my Cloaths and sit up all night by reason of a snake having got under my Pillow, which made me afraid I having no light to clear the bedd of him.

[Page 58th]   Thursday 4th.

This day William Pattie entred to school again at 11 AM. In the afternoon walking in the corn field I was surprised to see the Indian Corn so tawle, some of it being 12 foot high, and having five Ears of

Corn on Some of them which is generally the most that any one stalk bears, and there is two or three stalks in a hill and every hill is six feet at least one from another and some Gentlemen have the hills eight feet distance from one another, and there will be from four, to six Hundred grains in one eare, that grows from one grain planted.

FREIDAY 5TH.

Nothing remarcable.

SATURDAY 6TH.

Do. . . . Do.

SUNDAY 7TH.

This afternoon meeting accidentaly with a Gentleman here who was on his way to London I wrote my wife a few lines by him having wrote her fully 14th. June last but having omitted to insert the Coppy in it's proper pleace I now do it here before I insert the coppy of my Second Letter to her from this country.

Belvidera 14th. June 1774.

My Dearest Life

I wrote you from London on Wednesday 26th. Jany. last which Im hopefull came safe to hand, and found you and my dear Infants in perfect health, and am hopefull this will find both you and them in the same state, As I am at present and have been I bless God since I left you. You will remember [*Page 59*] when I wrote you last, I informed you that I was to go for Baltimore in Maryland, But I altred my design in that and came here it being a more healthy pleace. I sailed from London on Freiday the 4th. Feby. last, and aravied in Hampton roads in Virginia on the 27 Aprile, having been a Month of the time at Spithead in England. As to particulars of our Voyage &ca. it wou'd take up too much room here to insert it, But I have a Journal of every days transactions and remarcable occurances since the morning I left you which will be amusing to you when please God we are spared to meet, for I design to see & prepare a way for you all in this Country how soon I am able.—I shall now aquant you with my situation in this Country. I am now settled with on[e] Colonel Wm. Daingerfield Esqr. of Belvidera, on the Banks of the River Rappahannock about 160 Miles from the Capes or sea mouth, and seven Miles below the Toun of Fredericksburgh. My bussiness is to teach his Childreen to read write and figure. Edwin his oldest son about 8 years of [age] Bathurest his second 6 years of age & William his youngest son 4 years of age. He has also a Daugher whose name is Hanna Basset. I came to this pleace on Thursday 26th. May and next morning I received his three sons into my charge to teach, the two youngest boys I got in A:B:C, and the oldest just begun to syllab and I have now the two youngest spelling and the oldest reading. [*Page 60*] I am obliged to teach in the English method which was a litle aquard to me at first but now quite easy. I am also obliged to talk english the best I can, for Lady Daingerfield speacks nothing but high english, and the Colonel hade his Education in England and is a verry smart Man. As to my Agreement it is as follows Vizt. I am obliged to continue with Coll. Daingerfield for four years if he insists on it, and for teaching his own Childreen I have Bed, Board, washing and all kind of Cloaths during the above time, and for what schoolars

59 *Sunday 7th August 1774*

When I wrote you last, I informed you that I was to go for Baltimore in Maryland, But I altred my design in that and came here it being a more healthy pleace. I sailed from London on Friday the 4th Feby last, and arrived in Hampton roads in Virginia on the 27 Aprile, having been a Month of the time at Spithead in England; As to particulars of our voyage &ca it would take up too much room here to insert it. But I have a Journal of every days transz actions and remarkeable occurances since the morning I left you which will be amusing to you when pleased God we are spared to meet for I design to see & prepare a way for you all in this Country how soon I am able. ———— I shall now aquant you of my situation in this Country I am now settled with on Colonel Willm Daingerfield Esqr of Belvidera, on the Banks of the River Rappahannock about 160 Miles from the Capes or sea mouth, and seven Miles below the Town Fredericksburgh. My business is to teach his Children to read write and figure, Edwin his oldest son about 8 years of Bathurst his second 6 years of age & William his youngest son 4 years of age he has also a Daughter whose name is Hanna Bassit. I came to this pleace on Thursday 26th May and next morning I received his three sons into my charge to teach, the two youngest boys I got in A:B:C. and the oldest Just begun to Syllab and I have now the two youngest spelling and the oldest reading

Page 59 from original manuscript journal.

I can get more than his Childreen I have five shillings currancy per Quarter for each of them which is equall to four shillings Sterling, and I expect ten or twelve to school next week, for after I hade been here eight days and my abilities and my behavier sufficiently tried, the Colonel rode through the neighbouring Gentlemen & Planters in order to procure scollars for me, so that I hope in a short time to make something of it. And as I have no occasion to spend a farthing on myself every Shillg. I make shall be carefully remitted you, for your support and my Dear Infants. But I must be some time here before any thing can be done, for you know every thing must have a begining.

As to my living I eat at their own table, & our witualls are all Dressed in the english taste. We have for breackfast either Coffie or Jaculate, and warm [*Page 61*] loaf bread of the best floor, we have also at Table warm loaf bread of Indian corn, which is extreamly good but we use the floor bread always at breackfast. For Dinner smoack'd bacon or what we cal pork ham is a standing dish either warm or cold. When warm we have greens with it, and when cold we have sparrow grass. We have also either warm roast pigg, Lamb, Ducks, or chickens, green pease or any thing else they fancy. As for Tea there is none drunk by any in this Government since 1st. June last, nor will they buy a 2d. worth of any kind of east India goods, which is owing to the difference at present betwixt the Parliment of great Brittan and the North Americans about laying a tax on the tea; and I'm afraid if the Parliment do not give it over it will cause a total revolt as all the North Americans are determined to stand by one another, and resolute on it that they will not submit. I have the news paper sent me to school regularly every week by the Coll.—Our Family consists of the Coll. his Lady & four Childreen a housekeeper an overseer and myself all white. But how many blacks young and old the Lord only knows for I belive there is about thirty that works every day in the field besides the servants about the house; such as Gardner, livery men and pages, Cooks, washer & dresser, sewster and waiting girle. They wash here the whitest that ever I seed for they first Boyle all the Cloaths with soap, and then wash them, and I may put on clean linen every day if I please. My school is a neate [*Page 62*] little House 20 foot Long and 12 foot wide & it stands by itself at the end of an Avenue of planting about as far from the main house as Robt. Forbes's[66] is from the burn, and there comes a bonny black bairn every morning to clean it out and make my bed for I sleep in it by myself. I have a verry fine feather bed under me, and a pair of sheets, a thin fold of a Blanket and a Cotton bed spread is all my bed cloaths, and I find them Just enough. As for myself I supose you wou'd scarce know me now, there being nothing either brown, blew, or black about me but the head and feet, I being Dressed in short cloath Coat, vest Coat, and britches all made of white cotton without any lyning, and thread stockins & wearing my own hair curled round like a wigg. At present a suite of Cloaths costs five and twenty shillings here of making which I really think verry high.

I was Sunday last at Fredericksburgh at church and I then settled a safe Correspondance for your letters to come to me, and shall give you the proper directions below. As for myself I thank God I want for nothing that is necessarry, But it brings tears from my eyes to think of you and my Infants when at same time it is not in my power at present to help you. But how soon I am able you may depend upon it. [*Page 63*] I have little else to say at present; only may the great God who governs all things wisely suport you and my Infants, and guide and direct you in all your ways.

I shall write you again soon and when you write me direct my letters as follows Vizt. to John Harrower at the seat of Colonel Wm. Daingerfield Esqr. of Belvidera near Fredericksburgh on Rappahannock River Virginia; Then you must take half a sheet of paper and write another letter the Contents of which may be as follows Vizt. Gentlemen being desired by my husband to send his letters under cover to you, You will please foreward the inclosed by the first ship bound for any part in Virginia and charge Mr. Glassel Mercht. in Fredericksburgh with the expence you are at; I am yours &ca. signed A. H. After you have closed my letter and directed it as above, You will inclose it in the above, and direct it as follows To Messrs. Anderson & Horsburgh Merchts. in Glasgow. You must get some person to fold up your letters properly and on[e] who writes a clean Distinct hand to direct them. Pray write me verry particularly how it is with you and my Dr. Infants, likeways any thing that is remarcable in the Country. I shall conclude this with offering my Compts. to all enquiring freinds if I have any and my sinceer prayers both evening and morning for you & my Childreen. My Blessing to you all, is all at present from my Dearest Jewell your ever affte. Husband untill Death. Signed—John Harrower.

Addressed, to Mrs. John Harrower in Lerwick, Zetland.

[*Page 64th*]

2d. Letter from Virginia.

Belvidera 7 Augt. 1774.

My Dearest Life

I wrote you verry fully 14th. June last to which I refer you it being verry full, but meeting Accidentally Just now with a Gentleman bound to London, I have just time to write you a few lines while he is at Dinner to let you know that I am still in good health I thank God for it, and am hopefull this will find you and my Dr. Infants the same. I gave you verry full Directions in my last how to write me but in case this should come to hand before it, I shall here again repeat them—See Directions page 63.—[67]

If this or my other letter comes to hand before the Pacquet leaves Zetland for the last time this winter,[68] pray do not faill to write me verry fully by her. I have Just time to aquant you that I am settled here as a Schoolmaster and can really say with great truth that I never lived a genteel regulare life untill now. I shall write you again soon verry fully and untill then I am with my blessing to you my Dear and my Dear Infants, Your ever Affte. husbd. untill death—Signed—John Harrower.

Adressed, To Mrs. John Harrower, Lerwick, Zetland.

[*Page 65th*]   MUNDAY 8TH. AUGT. 1774.

Nothing remarcable.

TUESDAY 9TH.

Do. . . . Do.

WEDNESDAY 10TH.

Do. . . . Do.

THURSDAY 11TH.

This morning at 5 AM Coll. William Daingerfields youngest Son was baptized and was called John he being verry ill and not expected to live.[69]

FREIDAY 12TH.

Nothing remarcable.

SATURDAY 13TH.

Do. . . . Do.

SUNDAY 14TH.

Went to Church on Horseback, Text 14 Ver. 12 Chap. of the Hebrews.

MUNDAY 15TH.

Nothing remarcable.

TUESDAY 16TH.

Expecting a visit of one Mr. Kennedy an Edinburgher, a Cooper now in Fredericksburgh, I this day sent to Toun for a Quart of the best Vestindia Rum which cost me Eighteen pence Virginia Currancy.

WEDNESDAY 17TH.

This evening entred to school Thomas Brooks Mr. Spotswoods carpenter in order to learn writing and Arithmetick at nights and on Sundays.[70]

THURSDAY 18TH.

Nothing remarcable.

FREIDAY 19TH.

This day at noon Coll. Willm. Daingerfield finished his wheat Harvest by getting the last of it brought home & stacked.

[*Page 66th*]   SATURDAY 20TH. AUGT. 1774

Nothing remarcable.

SUNDAY 21ST.

At home teaching Brooks.

MUNDAY 22D.

This afternoon Coll. Daingerfield begun to sow wheat again for the next years crope. They sow their wheat here in the field where there Indian Corn is growing and ploughs it into the ground, so that the Corn and wheat both occopy the ground from this date untill January next and then the Corn is cut down.

TUESDAY 23D.

This day at noon was finished at one of Coll. Daingerfields Barns a new Machine for beating out of wheat. It is a circle of 60 feet diameter in the center of which their is a paul fixed in the ground from which there goes three beams that reach the outter edge of the great circle and betwixt the outer ends of them are fixt four rollers, each roller having 320 spokes in it, they are 6 feet long, vizt. the rollers, and goes round upon a floor of 3 Inch plank of 7 feet long from the outer edge of the great circle and round the outer ends of the floor plank there is a thin plank upon it's edge and round the inner edge the same which keeps in the wheat. The Machine is drawn round by 4 Horses and beats out 100 Bushels of wheat every day.[71] It was begun 1st. Instant.

WEDNESDAY 24TH.

Nothing remarcable.

THURSDAY 25TH.

Nothing remarcable.

FREIDAY 26TH.

Do. .... Do.

The threshing machine described by John Harrower as depicted on a medal presented to the inventor, John Hobday, by the Society for the Advancement of Useful Knowledge on June 15, 1774. Courtesy Virginia Historical Society.

SATURDAY 27TH.

Do. .... Do.

[*Page 67th*]   SUNDAY 28TH. AUGT. 1774

At home all day teaching Brooks.

MUNDAY 29TH.

Nothing remarcable.

TUESDAY 30TH.

Do. .. Do.

WEDNESDAY 31ST.

This forenoon Mrs. Daingerfield made her first appearance out of her Room since being delivered.

THURSDAY 1ST. SEPTR.

Nothing remarcable.

FREIDAY 2D.

Do. .. Do.

SATURDAY 3D.

Do. .. Do.

SUNDAY 4TH.

Do. .. Do.

MUNDAY 5TH.

Do. .. Do.

TUESDAY 6TH.

Do. .. Do.

WEDNESDAY 7TH.

Do. . . Do.

THURSDAY 8TH.

Do. . . Do.

FREIDAY 9TH.

Do. . . Do.

SATURDAY 10TH.

Do. . . Do.

SUNDAY 11.

Do. teaching Brooks. At 1 pm came Mr. Kennedy from Fredericks-burgh here to see me and after we had dined we ended the Quart of Rum I Bought 16th. Last Mo.

MUNDAY 12TH.

Nothing remarcable.

TUESDAY 13TH.

Returd. Dor. & Philop Edges.

[*Page 68th*]   WEDNESDAY 14TH. SEPT. 1774

Nill.

THURSDAY 15TH.

Do.

FREIDAY 16TH.

Do.

SATURDAY 17TH.

Do.

SUNDAY 18TH.

Do.

MUNDAY 19TH.

Began to cut corn tops & pul fodder.[72]

TUESDY 20TH.

Yearly fair at Fredericksbg.

WEDNESDAY 21ST.

Nil.

THURSDAY 22D.

Do.

FREIDAY 23D.

Do.

SATURDAY 24TH.

Lewis Richards left school.

SUNDAY 25TH.

Nil.

MUNDAY 26TH.

Do.

TUESDAY 27TH.

Do.

WEDNESDAY 28TH.

Do.

THURSDAY 29TH.

Do.

Freiday 30th.

Do.

Saturdy. 1st. Octr.

Do.

Sunday 2d.

Dined at Mr. Thos. Evans's.

Munday 3d.

Nil.

Tuesday 4th.

I Went to Fredericksbg. & seed a Horse Race for a Hundred Guineas, Gained by Mr. Fitchews Horse.

[*Page 69th*]   Wednesday 5th. Octr. 1774.

This day a Horse race at Fredericksburg for Fifty pound & it was gain'd by a Horse belonging to Coll. Tailo.

Thursday 6th.

This day a Horse race at Fredericksburg for Fifty pound, & it was gained by a Horse belonging to Mr. Fitchew.

Freiday 7th.

The race this day at Fredericksburg for Fifty pound was gained again by another Horse belonging to Mr. Fitchew.[73]

Saturday 8th.

This day the races at Fredericksburg was finished and this night finishes the Puppet shows, roape dancings &ca. which has continowed every night this week in town. I only seed the purse of a Hundred Guineas run for, and that day I hade the Misfortune to have my Horse, saddle and bridle stole from me, while I was doing some bussiness in town. And I never could hear, nor get any intelligence of either of them again.

SUNDAY 9TH.

Nothing remarcable.

MUNDAY 10TH.

Lewis Richards returned.

TUESDAY 11TH.

Lucy Pattie came to School.

WEDNESDAY 12TH.

Nil.

THURSDAY 13TH.

Do.

FREIDAY 14TH.

Do.

SATURDAY 15TH.

Finished Fodder &ca. Do.

SUNDAY 16TH.

This day Mrs. Daingerfield was Churched at Fredericksburgh.

[*Page 70th*]   MUNDAY 17TH. OCTR. 1774.

Nil.

TUESDAY 18TH.

Do.

WEDNESDAY 19TH.

Do.

THURSDAY 20TH.

Do.

FREIDAY 21ST.

Do.

SAT. 22D.

Do.

SUNDAY 23D.

At church but there was no sermon only prayers. This day I carried home a Westcoat with a silver sprig through a strip'd white satine & Padasoy silk, which I had formerly bought made as it was being nothing worse than new for 8/6 Virginia Currancy, and a Brass Inkholder with a penknife in it bought at 1/6 Cy.

MUNDAY 24TH.

Nil.

TUESDAY 25TH.

Do.

WEDNESDAY 26TH.

Do.

THURSDAY 27TH.

I eat green Pease at dinner.

FREIDAY 28TH.

Nil.

SATURDAY 29TH.

Do.

SUNDAY 30TH.

At home teaching Brooks.

Munday 31st.

This morning two Carpenters was put to new weather board my house on the outside with featherage plank, and to new plaster it on the Inside with shell lime.

[*Page 71st*]   ### Tuesday 1st. Novr. 1774

This day Coll. William Daingerfield finished sowing his Wheat, having sown in all this year 160½ bushels.[74]

This day I eat extream good green Pease they being the second croap this season. In the afternoon they began to gather new corn & brot. home 8 Barrels at night from 1000 Corn hills.

Wednesday 2d.

Nil.

Thursday 3d.

Do.

FRIDAY 4TH.

Yesterday at 12 Lewis Richards left school.

SATURDAY 5TH.

Nil.

SUNDAY 6TH.

At home teaching Brooks.

MUNDAY 7TH.

Nil.

TUESDAY 8TH.

Do.

WEDNESDAY 9TH.

Do.

THURSDAY 10TH.

Do.

FREIDAY 11.

Do.

SATURDAY 12TH.

SUNDAY 13TH.

At home teaching Brook[s].

MUNDAY 14TH.

Nil.

TUESDAY 15TH.

Do.

WEDNESDAY 16TH.

Do.

THURSDAY 17TH.

Do.

FREIDAY 18TH.

Do.

SATURDAY 19TH.

Do.

[Page 72d]   SUNDAY 20TH. NOVR. 1774.

At home all day teaching Tho. Brooks.

MUNDAY 21ST.

Nil.

TUESDAY 22D.

Do.

WEDNESDAY 23D.

Do.

THURSDAY 24TH.

Do.

FREIDAY 25TH.

Do.

SATURDAY 26TH.

This day at Church & heard Sermon by Mr. Muree[75] his text was in Hebrows 13th Chap: & 18th. Verse. Bought a hanging lock for my Chest at 7½ Currancy.

Recd. from Colonel Daingerfield New Coat and veastcoat of Claret couler'd Duffel.

SUNDAY 27TH.

The being at Church &ca. marked 26 Inst. was only this day.

MUNDAY 28TH.

Nil.

TUESDAY 29TH.

Do.

WEDNESDAY 30TH.

Do.

THURSDAY 1ST. DECEMBER.

Do.

FREIDAY 2D.

Do.

SATURDAY 3D.

Do.

SUNDAY 4TH.

Put on a pair new Shoes.

MUNDAY 5TH.

TUESDAY 6TH.

Wrote home.—3d. Letter from Virginia.

[*Page 73d*]

Belvidera 6th. Decr. 1774.

My Dearest Life,

Since my aravil here I wrote you 14th June & 7th. Augt. last to both which I shall partly refer you. I now rite you with a shaking hand and a feeling heart to enquir of your and my Dr. Infants welfare, this being the return of the day of the year on which I was obliged to leave you and my Dr. Infants early in the morning which day will be ever remembred by me with tears untill it shall please God to grant us all a happy meeting again. I trust in the mercies of a good God this will find you and my Dr. Infants in perfect health as I am and have been ever since I came here, for neither the heat in summer nor what I have as yet felt of the cold in Winter gives me the least uneaseiness I thank God for it. About 20 days ago I only laid aside my summer dress, and put on a suite of new Claret Coulerd Duffle neatly mounted but no lyning in the Coat only faced in the breasts. I wrote you in my first letter, that I was designed Please God to prepare a way for you and my Infants in this Country; And I begg youll give me your thoughts fully upon it, in your first letter after receipt of this with respect to your moving here. If you do your method must be thus; Take your Passage to Leith, from thence go to Glasgow and from that to Greenock where you will ship for this Country. But this you are not [*Page 74*] to attemp untill I have your thoughts upon it and I send you a recomendation to a Mercht. in Glasgow and cash to bear your expences. I have as yet only ten Scollars One of which is both Deaff and Dumb and his Father pays me ten shilling per Quarter for him he has been now five Mos. with [me] and I have brought him tolerably well and understands it so far, that he can write mostly for any thing he wants and understands the value of every figure, and can work single addition a little. He is aboutt fourteen years of age. Another of them is a young man a house Carpenter who Attends me every night with candle light and every Sunday that I don't go to

Church for which he pays me fourty shillings a year. He is Carpenter for a gentleman who lives two miles from me and has Thirty pound a year, free bedd & board.

The Colls. Childreen comes on pretty well. The Eldest is now reading verry distinctly in the Psalter according to the Church of England and the other two boys ready to enter into it; The Col. and his Lady being extreamly well satisfied with my Conduct in every respect; on 31st. Jully last Mrs. Daingerfield was delivd. of a fourth son who is now my nameson. I am now verry impatient to hear from you and I [beg?] of you not to slip a Packqut without writting me, Accord to the directions I formerly sent you which I shall again repeat in this [*Page 75*] for fear of my former letters being miscarried which I hope not; The next time [I] write you I hope to be able to make you a small remittance.

I wou'd have at this time wrote your Brother Mr. Craigie,[76] for I truely belive his private good wishes to me was always sinceer, But I want to hear from you first by which I hope to learn how every one's pulse in your place beats towards me and his among the rest, which I hope you'll not fail to take notice of.—I now as far as my sheet of paper will allow me, for your Amusement and information, shall write you some of the news of this Western World, and first with respect to my self. Know that I have not drunk a dish of Tea this six Mos. past, nor have I drunk a dram of plain spirits[77] this seven Mos. past, nor have I tasted broth or any kind of supping mate for the above time unless three or four times some soup; Notwithstanding I want for nothing that I cou'd desire, and am only affraid of getting fatt, tho we seldom eat here but twice a day. For Breackfast we have always Coffie with plenty of warm loaf bread and fine butter. At 12 oClock when I leave School, I have as much good rum toddie as I chuse to drink, and for Dinner we have plenty of roast & boyld and good strong beer, but seldom eat any supper. There has been a hote War here this last summer betwixt the fronteer Countys of this Collony and the united tribes [*Page 76*] of the Shawaneses, Delewars, Mingoes, & Tawa Indians settled on the otherside of the Banks of the Ohio.

On Munday morning 10th. Octr. last a Deccisive Battle was fought at the mouth of the great Canhawa[78] Betwixt 150 of Augusta County troops under the Command of Coll. Chas. Lewis 300 of the troops belonging to Botitourt, Bedford & Fincastle

County, Under the Command of Coll. Fleming, and Coll. Field; The Battle began half an hour after sun up and continoued verry hot until after noon, when the above Indians being above 800 in number were put to flight. In this Action were killed the above Coll. Chas. Lewis & Coll. Field, Four Captains three subalterns and 44 private men. Coll. Fleming was wounded three Captains four subalterns and 79 private men. The same evening after the Battle an express aravied at the Camp from Lord John Dunmore Governour of Virginia for this Division of the Army to Joyne him, he being then 75 Miles further up the Ohio on the Indian side with 600 More of the troops belonging to the foresaid Countys, he then knowing nothing of the Battle. Next day this part of the Army decamp'd and when they hade Joyn'd His Lodsp. All the Army march'd foreward in order to Burn and destroy the whole Indian Touns; But when they were within three Miles of them, The Indians came out naked [*Page* 77] as they were born and Begged for Mercy and peace, they having lost above double the number of men that we did in the late engagement. Accordingly peace was granted them on the following terms Vizt. 1st. They are to deliver up all the white prisoners they have, next they are to deliver up somany of their principall men of each nation, to be keept as hostages for their good behavour in time to come, lastly they are to pay the whole expence of the war in land at three pound per M Acres. So much for Indian news.

You no doubt have heard of the present disturbs. Betwixt Great Britain and the Collonys in N. America, Owing to severall Acts of Parliment latly made greatly infringing the rights and Liberties of the Americans, and in order to enforce these Acts, The Harbour and Toun of Boston are at present blockt up by a fleet and armie under the Command of Genl. Gage. The Americans are determined to Act with Caution and prudence in this affair, and at same time are resolved not to lose an inch of their rights or liberties, nor to submit to these Acts. And in order to enforce a repeal of them, A Generall Congress was held at Philadelphia by Delegates from the following Provinces Vizt. New Hampshire, Massachusetts Bay, Rode Island & Providence Plantations, Connicticut, New York, New Jersey, [*Page 78*] Pennsylvania, The Countys of Newcastle, Kent, and Sussex on Delewar, Maryland, Virginia, North Carolina, and South Carolina. The

Delegates were chosen from the Houses of Burges of each of the above Collonys and met on the 5th. Septr. last and continued sitting untill the last of Octr. And it is resolved that they will allow no goods to be imported into America from Great Britain, Ireland or any of the Islands thereto belonging after the 1st. Inst. Nor will they export from America to Great Britain or Ireland or any of the Islands thereto belonging any goods after the 1st. Decr. 1775 during which time any that are indebted to Great Britain may pay up their ballances. Ma[n]y and pretty are the resolves of August Assembly but room wou'd fail me here to insert them. By the Congress the Bostonians are desired not to Leave the Toun nor to give any offence to Genl. Gage or the troops under his Command, But if he or they offers to commit the least Hostielyties in order to enforce any to the Obedience of these Acts, they are to repeal force by force and the Bostonians can raise in their Collony on 24 Hours warning ods of 60 M. men well disiplined and all readdy provided with arms and amunition. And the resolves of the Congress every one of the above Collonys and each man in every Collony are determined to abide by. And it is my oppinion that the laboring [*Page 79*] part and poor of Boston, are as well supplied at present by controbutions sent free to them from the other Collonys as when their trade was oppen. Mr. Daingerfield this year for his own hand gives them fifty Bushels of wheat and One Hundred Bushels of Indian Corn, By which ye may Judge of the rest.[79]

The 19th. August last, Mr. Daingerfield finished his wheat hearvest and began to plow and sow wheat again for the next crop 22 said Mo. and after sowing 260 Bushels finished it the 1st. of Novr. They are now gathering Indian corn of which he will have better than 4000 Bushels 3000 of which he will Use for his Nigers and horses, the rest for sale; So much for American and Plantation news the Veracity of which you may depend upon and may show the same to any of your freinds or well wishers.

Your directions for me is to Jno. Harrower at the seat of Coll. Willm. Daingerfield Esqr. of Belvidera near Fredericksburgh Rappahannock River Virginia, and then inclose it in a letter to Messrs. Anderson and Horseburgh Merchts. in Glasgow and desire them to foreward the same under Cover to Mr. John Glassel Mert. in Fredericksbg. their Correspondent who will pay all charges for my Accott.—Pray my Dearest let me know [*Page 80*] what my Dr. Boys and Girle are doing. I hope Jock & George are still at school and I begg of you to strain every nerve to keep them at it untill I am able to assist you, for he who has got education will always gain Bread and to spare, & that in a genteel way in some place or other of the World. I supose Betts is at home with yourself, but pray keep her tight to her seam & stockin, and any other Housold affairs that her years are capable of and do not bring her up to Idleness or play or going about from house to house which is the first inlet in any of the sex to laziness and vice. Send me an Accot. of their Ages from the Bible which ye may do verry short by saying Jo: Born—day Novr. 1762 Geo: Born &ca.[80]

I yet hope (please God) if I am spared, some time to make you a Virginian Lady among the woods of America which is by far more pleasent than the roaring of the raging seas round abo't Zetland, And yet to make you eat more wheat Bread in your old age than what you have done in your Youth. But this I must do by carefullness, industry and a Close Application to Bussines, which ye may take notice of in this letter I am doing Sunday as well as Saturday nor will I slip an honest method nor an hour whereby I can [*Page 81*] gain a penny for yours & my own advantage.

There grows here plenty of extream fine Cotton which after being pict clean and readdy for the cards is sold at a shilling the pound; And I have at this time, a great high Gir[l]e Carline as Black as the D - - s. A - - se spinning some for me for which I must pay her three shillings the pound for spinning it for she must do it on nights or on Sunday for any thing I know notwithstanding she's the Millers wife on the next plantation. But Im determined to have a webb of Cotton Cloath According to my own mind, of which I hope you and my infants shall yet wear apart; I cou'd write to you for a week for it gives me pleaser while I am writting to you, But as room fails me I must conclude with offering my good wishes to your Brothr., Mr. & Mrs. Vance,[81] Mr. & Mrs. Forbes and Mr. Ferguson[82] if deserving at your hand with my Compts. to all who asks for me. And my sinceer prayers to God for you and my Dr. Childreen & belive me to be ever while I have breath, My dearest Jewell, your Affet. husbd. till death.

Signed J. H.

Addressed to Mrs. John Harrower in Lerwick Zetland By Edinburgh, North Britain.

[*Page 82d*]   WEDNESDY. 7TH. DECR. 1774.

THURSDAY 8TH.

Nil.

FREIDAY 9TH.

Do.

SATURDAY 10TH.

This day after 12 Oclock rode to Town and delivd. my letter dated 6th. Inst. to Mr. John Glassell to be forewarded to Britain per first ship. Bought 1 Pad Lock at 1/ Curcy. & 1 Dozn. vest buttons silver plated at 1/ Curcy. & pocket expence 9d. Curcy.

SUNDAY 11TH.

At home, hard frost Wind N.W.

MUNDAY 12TH.

Hard frost continous Wind W.

TUESDAY 13TH.

This day at 12 Oclock it began to snow verry fast for the 1st. time this season.

WEDNESDY. 14TH.

This day Mr. Daingerfield hade 35 Hoggs Killed weighting at an average about 150 lb. and they are to serve for salt Beacon untill the return of next year this time. All the Hams and shoulders are cured with salt peter. Sold ½ dozn. horn Buttons at 3 ¾.

THURSDAY 15TH.

This afternon I took Accott. of the pork.

FREIDAY 16TH.

Nil.

SATURDAY 17TH.

Do.

SUNDAY 18TH.

At home teaching Brooks.

MUNDAY 19TH.

Nil.

TUESDAY 20TH.

Last night I dreamt that my wife came to me here, and told me she had sent Johnnie & Bettie to Deall to stay & left George in the house with M. J. the servant.[83]

[*Page 83d*] WEDNESDAY 21ST. DECR. 1774.

Thursday 22d.

Nil.

Freiday 23d.

Do.

Saturday 24th.

Do.

Sunday 25th.

Christmas day, stayed at home all day along with the Overseer & Childreen because I hade no saddle to go to the Church with. In the Morning the Coll. Ordred up to school two Bottles of the best Rum and some suggar for me.

Munday 26th.

This forenoon the Coll. wou'd have me to take his saddle and ride to Toun and Amuse myself, and when I was going gave me Six Shillings for pocket money.

I went to Toun and Dined in a private house & after buying 1½ Dozn. Mother of Pearle buttons for my white morsyld Vest I return'd home in the evening.

Tuesday 27th.

St. Johns day. This day a Grand Lodge in Toun, And the whole went to Church in their Clothing & heard Sermon.

Wednesday 28th.

At home.

Thursday 29th.

I began to keep school.

FREIDAY 30TH.

This day there was severall Gentlemen from Fredericksburgh here at Dinner with whom I dined.

SATURDAY 31ST.

Nothing remarcable.

[*Page 84th*]   SUNDAY 1ST. JANY. 1775.

Nil.

MUNDAY 2D.

Do.

TUESDAY 3D.

Do.

WEDNESDAY 4TH.

Do.

THURSDAY 5TH.

Do.

FREIDAY 6TH.

Do.

SATURDAY 7TH.

Do.

SUNDAY 8TH.

Do.

MUNDAY 9TH.

Do.

TUESDAY 10TH.

This day Thos. Brooks who has atten[d]ed ever[y] night and on Sundays left school being obliged to go 40 miles up the country to work. At same time he gave me an order on Coll. Daingerfield for £1. 10. 8d. Currcy. of which £1. 5. 2 was for teaching him.

WEDNESDAY 11TH.

Nil.

THURSDAY 12TH.

FREIDAY 13TH.

SATURDAY 14TH.

Yesterday Miss Lucy Gaines[84] went up the Country with a Brother of Law of her's who came for her Express to go to her Mother, so at [this?] point no Housekeeper.

[*Page 85th*]　　　SUNDAY 15TH. JANY. 1775.

MUNDAY 16.

Nil.

TUESDAY 17TH.

Do.

WEDNESDAY 18TH.

Do.

THURSDAY 19TH.

Do.

FREIDAY 20TH.

Do.

SATURDAY 21ST.

Some time ago I having got a present of piece of Lead coul[er?]d Cloath from Miss Lucy Gaines I got made in a Vest by Kidbeck[85] the Taylor for which I have this day paid him 3/1½ Curcy.

SUNDAY 22D.

This day at Church in Town and heard Mr. Maree preach Text 2d. Cors. 4 Chap: & 18th. Verse.

MUNDAY 23D.

Nil.

TUESDAY 24TH.

Do.

WEDNESDAY 25.

Do.

THURSDAY 26.

Do.

FREIDAY 27.

Do.

SATURDAY 28.

Do.

SUNDAY 29TH.

At Home. Do.

MUNDAY 30TH.

Do.

TUESDAY 31ST.

At 1 pm yesterday Jas. & Wm. Porters, Sons of Mr. William Porter Mercht.[86] in Fredericksbg. came here to School.

[*Page 86th*]   FEBRUARY 1ST. 1775.

Nil.

THURSDAY 2D.

Do.

FREIDAY 3D.

Do.

SATURDAY 4TH.

Do.

SUNDAY 5TH.

Do.

MUNDAY 6TH.

Do.

TUESDAY 7TH.

Do.

WEDNESDAY 8TH.

Do.

THURSDAY 9TH.

Do.

FREIDAY 10TH.

Do.

SATURDAY 11TH.

Do.

SUNDAY 12TH.

At Home. Do.

MUNDAY 13TH.

Do.

TUESDAY 14TH.

This day the Coll. on finding more wheat left among the straw then should be blamed Mr. Lewis the Overseer for his carelessness, upon which Mr. Lewis seem'd verry much enraged for being spoke to and verry sawcily threw up all the keys he hade in charge and vent off; upon which the Coll. sent for me and delivered me the keys of the Barn and begged I would assist him in his bussiness untill he got another Overseer.

[*Page 87th*]   FEBY. 15TH.

This morning the Coll. sent to scholl for me, and begg'd me to go to Snowcreek Barn and deliver the wheat that was there first to the Vessel who was come to receive the whole of it. She was a Schooner of 120 Tun Mrs. name Jno. Lurtey.[87]

16TH.

This day employd. delivering Wheat.

17TH.

This day employed as yesterday.

SATURDAY 18TH.

Employd delivg. Wheat.

SUNDAY 19TH.

At home all day.

MUNDAY 20TH.

Empld. delivering Wheat.

TUESDAY 21.

Empld. as Yesterday. This day the Coll. engaged a young man for an Overseer whose name is Anthony Fraser.[88]

WEDNESDY. 22D.

Empld. delivering Wheat.

THURSDAY 23D.

This day finised trading out wheat, also delivered the last of it having delivered One thousand five hundred Bushels and 240 Bushels formerly delivd. by Mr. Lewis which with 260 Bushels sown makes 2000 Bushels besides serving the Famely and some bushels sold to people who works on the plantation.

FREIDAY 24TH.

At school.

SATURDAY 25TH.

Nil.

SUNDAY 26TH.

Do.

[*Page 88th*]   MUNDAY FEBY. 27TH. 1775.

This day Mr. Fraser came here and entred to take his charge as Overseer, and he is to have his bed in the school along with me. He appears to be a verry quiet young man and has hade a tolerable education. His Grandfather came from Scotland.

TUESDAY 28TH.

Nil.

WEDNESDY. 1ST MARCH.

Yesterday Coll. Daingerfield began to plow his ground for planting his croop of Indian corn this year.

THURSDAY 2D.

Nil.

FREIDAY 3D.

This day two hands Employed in the Garden sowing early pease &ca.

SATURDAY 4TH.

Nil.

SUNDAY 5TH.

At Home.

MUNDAY 6TH.

Nil.

TUESDAY 7TH.

This day came here a Charriot with two old Ladys and a young Miss Daughter to one of the old Ladys and a Gentleman on horseback all from Williamsburg. The young Ladys Mama being extreamly ill with the Dropsy &ca.

WEDNESDAY 8TH.

Nil.

THURSDAY 9TH.

Do.

[*Page 89th*]   FREIDAY 10TH. MARCH 1775.

This Night the young Ladys Mama died her[e] and none knew it until the morning notwithstanding her Daughter and a Niger waiting maid was in the room all night.[89]

SATURDAY 11TH.

This night I sat up all night with the Corps in Company with Miss Lucy Gaines, Miss Molly White and Mr. Frazer our Overseer.

SUNDAY 12TH.

At Sunset this evening the Corps being drest in a Calico Goun and white apron was put in a black Walnut Coffin lined with Flanen and pinchback handles. The corps has also a sheet round them; I sat up this night also in Company with the former young Ladies and Mr. Heely[90] Schoolmaster at Mr. Spotswoods.

MUNDAY 13TH.

At 10 AM I screwed down the lid of the Coffin and in company with Mr. Frazer and John McDearman[91] we put it on a Chair Carriage which was drove by a Niger to Snow Creek grave Yard. The Coll. & we accompaning the Corps ther where we put them in the Grave which was betwixt five and six foot deep and filled the grave half up with earth and then overlaid it with plank and so left it.

[Page 90th] TUESDAY 14TH. MARCH 1775.

This forenoon came here Mr. Man Page's[92] Coach with 4 or 5 Gentlemen in it and after dinner they in Compy. with the Coll. his Lady and the daughter of the deceased went to the grave & heard the service of the dead read by one Mr. Wilson[93] after which the grave was fully closed up.

WEDNESDAY 15TH.

Nil.

THURSDAY 16.

Wind at N.W. At 5 pm it began to blow very hard and continued so all night with frost.

FREIDAY 17TH.

Wind as yesterday. From 4 to 7 AM it blowed excessive hard so that it blow'd in the gavel of a brick house here call'd the Turky howse. From 7 AM moderate weather.

SATURDAY 18TH.

Last night a very keen frost so that all the fruit that is blossom'd is in danger of being killed by it. Same day I wrote Mr. Samuel Edge the following letter Vizt.

Sir

When I hade the pleasure of seeing [you] on the 4th. Feby. last at your howse you then told me you was to be in Town the week after, and proposed calling here in your way home, in order to pay me the twenty shillings as agreed on; but since have heard *[Page 91]* nothing from you. Nothing but the real necessity for some books (which I greatly want) Oblidges me now to trouble you with this, hopping if it is any ways convenient for you, that you will send the cash per the bearer (and if required) how soon time will permit me to see you shall give you an ample discharge. My Compliments to yourself Mrs. Edge and Miss Sally[94] and am &ca.

SUNDAY 19TH.

Nil.

MUNDAY 20TH.

Do.

TUESDAY 21ST.

Do.

WEDNESDAY 22D.

Do.

THURSDAY 23D.

Do.

FREIDAY 24TH.

Do.

SATURDAY 25TH.

At noon went to Newpost to see Mr. Martin Heely Schoolmaster for Mr. Spotswood's Children, and after Dinner I spent the afternoon with him in conversation & hearing him play the Fiddle. He also made a Niger come & play on an Instrument call'd a Barrafou.[95] The body of it is an oblong box with the mouth up & stands on four sticks put in bottom, & cross the [top?] is laid 11 lose sticks upon [which?] he beats.

[Page 92d]   SUNDAY 26TH. MARCH 1775.

At 9 AM set out on horseback for Mount Church in Caroline County in Company with Mr. Richards, Mrs. Richards, Mr. Martin Heely, Mr. Anthony Frazer and Miss Lucy Gaines. And heard Mr. Waugh[96] preach his text being the 1st. V. of the 12th. Chapter of Ecclesiastes. After which we all returned to Mr. Richards before 3 pm where we Dined & spent the afternoon. From Belvidera to Mount Church is 10 Miles.

MUNDAY 27TH.

Nil.

TUESDAY 28TH.

Do.

WEDNESDAY 29TH.

Do.

THURSDAY 30TH.

Do.

FREIDAY 31ST.

Do.

SATURDAY 1ST. APRILE.

At 6 pm Mr. Martin Heely Schoolmaster at Newpost for Mr. Spotswoods Childreen came here to pay me a Visite and staid with me all night.

SUNDAY 2D.

At home all the day.

MUNDAY 3D.

Nil.

TUESDAY 4TH.

Do.

WEDNESDAY 5TH.

Do.

THURSDAY 6TH.

Do.

FREIDAY 7TH.

Do.

SATURDAY 8TH.

At 3 pm went to Mr. Becks the Taylors & spent the afternoon.

[*Page 93d*]   SUNDAY 9TH. APRILE 1775.

This day a good number of Company dined her[e] among which was Mr. & Mrs. Porter from Town, who heard their Eldest Son read and seemed verry well pleased with his performance since he came to me; Myself at home all day.

MUNDAY 10TH.

Nil.

TUESDAY 11TH.

Do.

WEDNESDAY 12TH.

Do.

THURSDAY 13TH.

Do.

FREIDAY 14TH.

This being good Freiday, I broke up school for Easter Holly days, and the Colls. three sons went to Town with Mr. Porter's two sons this forenoon. I went a money hunting but catc'd none.[97]

SATURDAY 15TH.

This forenoon I went a Money Hunting again an other way but hade no better sucess then yesterday. This afternoon Mr. Frazer went up the Country to see his Mother and friends, and I give out corn for him, untill he returns again.

SUNDAY 16TH.

At home all day which owing to my not having a saddle of my own, and it being too far to go on foot to Church & return again on foot the same day, which Mr. Frasers absence wou'd Occassion me to do. The distance from this to Town being seven miles. Recd. a broke Sett Stock buckle from the Coll. in a present.

[Page 94th]   MUNDAY 17TH. APRILE 1775.

At 8 AM I rode to Town in order to see the boys and Amuse myself fore some hours. On my Aravel in Town the first thing I got to do was to dictate & write a love letter from Mr. Anderson,[98] to one Peggie Dewar at the Howse of Mr. John Mitchel[99] at the Wilderness. After that I went to Mr. John Glassell's store to enquire for letters from home but found none; here I mett with the Coll. who gave me two pair brown thread stockins for my summers wear. At 2 pm I dined with him in Mr. Porters, & soon after Returned home.

TUESDAY 18TH.

At home all day.

WEDNESDY. 19TH.

At 1 pm The boys retd. from Town & Mr. Porters two sons with them.

THURSDY. 20TH.

This morning all the boys came to school again at their Usual hour. On tuesday last was missed out of the pasture a breeding Mare. Search being made fore her by the Overseer he found this afternoon the Neiger fellow who hade rode her off and after riding her about 24 Miles from the Plantation turned her loose in the high road. He is a Blacksmith by trade & belongs to and works at a Plantation of Mr. Corbins,[100] and after he hade confessed the fact Mr. Frazer ower Overseer stript him to the [skin?] and gave him 39 laches with Hickry switches that being the highest the Law allows at one Wheeping.

[Page 96th]   FREIDAY 21ST. APRILE 1775.

Nil.

SATURDAY 22D.

At 3 pm went to New Post where the Coll. and severall Gentlemen hade been all day hauling a Sene net and hade catch'd a good deall herrings and white fish; but at noon their nett got foul of some driven tree at bottom & continued so untill I went off in a canoe & got it clear'd.

SUNDAY 23D.

At home all day.

MUNDAY 24TH.

This morning the Coll. began to have his Indian Corn planted which they do in following maner Vizt. The plowers plow three furrows close together from one end of the field to the other, the midle furrow of each three being 6 feet distance from the middle of the next three and so on from the one side of the field to the other. Then they run one furrow across the field and at 6 feet distance another and so on in streight lines from the one end of the field to the other which leaves the whole field like a dam brod.[101] Then the Neigers drop the corn in every square and at same time with a strock of their How cover the[m]. The grown betwixt the furrow are brocke up Afterwds. at Liesure with the Ploughs without any Damage to the corne. But the best method is when the ploughs is lay off the ground withe one furrow a Neiger ought to follower every Plough drop the corn & imediatly cover it up. Some are now done planting of corn. Last night Mr. Frazer found the Mare that was rode off & brought her home.

[*Page 97th*]   TUESDAY 25TH. APRILE 1775.

Nil.

WEDNESDAY 26TH.

Do.

THURSDAY 27TH.

Do.

Freiday 28th.

This day by an express from Boston we are informed of an engagement betwixt the British troops and the Bostonians, in which the former were repuls'd with loss, but no particulars as yet.[102]

Saturday 29th.

This day there was at Fredericksburgh about 600 men under Arms composed of the independant companys of severall Counties. They designed to have marched to Williamsburg & to have made the Governor deliver back some poweder he caused to be Clandestintly carried off, but was prevented by an express from the speacker with advice that the Governor was readdy to give it up on ten minutes warning.[103]

Sunday 30th.

At home all day.

Munday 1st. May.

Nil.

TUESDAY 2D.

Do.

WEDNESDAY 3D.

This day the Coll. bought and recd. ten Bushels of Spans. Salt for ten bushels Indian corn. At noon the Colls. Nigers finished planting Indian Corn having planted about 300 Acres of land, which took about 25 Bushels of sead.

THURSDAY 4TH.

Nil.

[*Page 98th*]   FREIDAY 5TH. MAY 1775.

Nil.

SATURDAY 6TH.

This afternoon I planted 41 Hills of grownd with Cotton seed.

SUNDAY 7TH.

At 2 houses this day seeking money that was owing me but got none.

MUNDAY 8TH.

This mor[n]ing I planted 22 Hills of grownd with Water Mellon and Mush Mellon Seed. This afternoon I eat ripe strawberries.

TUESDAY 9TH.

Nil.

WEDNESDY. 10TH.

Do.

THURSDAY 11TH.

Do.

FREIDAY 12TH.

Do.

SATURDAY 13TH.

At noon went to town on foot, and gave in my Sett Stock Buckle to Jas. Brown[104] to mend, also a Sett Hair pin of Miss Lucy Gaines's. I went & seed the Independant Compy. Exercise & then walked home in the evening.

SUNDAY 14TH.

At 8 AM sett off for Church on foot and was in Town above an Houre before Church time, heard Mr. Mayree Preach his text Gl. Eple. Jas. 2d. C. 19th. V. I walked home again and was done dinner at ½ an houre past 2 pm.

MUNDAY 15.

This afternoon I planted Water Melons and Mush Melons.

TUESDAY 16TH.

Nil.

WEDNESDAY 17TH.

This forenoon I seed some of my Cotton planted 6th. Inst. above the ground.

[*Page 99th*]   THURSDAY 18TH. MAY 1775.

Nil.

FREIDAY 19TH.

Do.

SATURDAY 20TH.

This day I wrote the following letter to Saml. Edge for Twenty Shillings that has been due me since the 25th. Novr. 1774.

Mr. Samuel Edge

Sir—I wrote you 18th. March last requesting you then to send me per the Bearer then sent, the twenty shillings you are indebted to me, which mony. you promised to have paid a Month before that time. Notwithstanding of which I have neither seen or heard from you since, which to me appears some what Strange.

On Saturday last I was informed you intended to send me a wild Goose hunting by giving me a Draught on another. But if any one is owing you I do not chuse to demand the debt; Therefore I hereby aquant you that I will not accept a draught upon none; Therefore I am hopefull you will now send the money by the bearer hereof as I really have pressing occassion for it and cannot be longer without it, having neither stock nor store here to raise money with to purchass what I really cannot be without. Your complyance to the above will greatly oblige and wherein I can serve you may freely command Sir yours &ca.

Signed J H.

Addressed to Mr. Samuel Edge—Overseer.

This afternoon I was invited to a Gentlemans house in order to eat plenty of ripe Cheeries.

[*Page 100th*]   SUNDAY 21ST. MAY 1775.

This day I hade sent me a present from Mrs. Porter in Fredg. two silk Vestcoats and two pair cotton britches all of them having been but verry little wore by Mr. Porter.

MUNDAY 22D.

Nil.

TUESDAY 23D.

Do.

WEDNESDAY 24TH.

Do.

THURSDAY 25TH.

Do.

FREIDAY 26TH.

Do.

SATURDAY 27TH.

This afternoon I rode to Town and bought at Mr. Porters Store 2 handkerchiefs and one Yd Bedd Tyke at 2/2d. Curcy. being all 5/2d. Curcy. At same time recd. a letter from my Wife dated 1st. March 1775. It came undercover to Mr. John Glassell Mercht. in Toun and cost me 1/3d. Curcy. At same time recd. from Thos. Anderson a pair new Shoes on the Colls. Accott.

SUNDAY 28TH.

Nil.

MUNDAY 29TH.

Do.

TUESDAY 30TH.

Do.

WEDNESDAY 31ST.

Do.

THURSDAY 1ST. JUNE.

Do.

FREIDAY 2D.

SATURDAY 3D.

At 9 AM. Mr. Porter's two son's was sent for, and they went to Toun to keep Whitesuntide holliday.

[*Page 101st*]   SUNDAY 4TH. JUNE 1775.

Nil.

MUNDY. 5TH.

Do.

TUESDAY 6TH.

Do.

WEDNESDY. 7TH.

Began to keep school again.

THURSDY. 8TH.

Mr. Porters two sons retd.

FREIDAY 9TH.

Nil.

SATURDAY 10TH.

Do.

SUNDAY 11TH.

This day I put on a pair new Shoes, and a pair new brown thread Stockins. Rod to Church and heard Mr. Marye preach, his text was in Roms. 8th. Chap: & 16 V.

MUNDAY 12TH.

Nil.

TUESDAY 13TH.

Do.

WEDNESDAY 14TH.

Do.

THURSDAY 15TH.

Do.

FREIDAY 16TH.

This day at 9 AM Colo. Daingerfield set out for his Qr. doun the Country at Chickahommanie to receive his Cash for the last years produce of said plantation from John Miller his Overseer there.[105]

SATURDAY 17TH.

Nil.

SUNDAY 18TH.

This day at 10 AM went to John Patties and recd. 6/ for teaching his William ¼ of a year and from [thence?] to Thomas Evans's and recd. 20/ for teaching his Daughtr. Sarah for one year.

[*Page 102d*]   MUNDAY 19TH. JUNE 1775.

This morning recd. my Shoes from Mr. Anderson half soled at 3/6. Same day in the afternoon they began to cut down Wheat.

TUESDAY 20TH.

Nil.

WEDNESDAY 21ST.

Do.

THURSDAY 22D.

Do.

FREIDAY 23D.

Do.

SATURDAY 24TH.

This day I went to Toun at noon & paid 5/ for mending the Sett Stock Buckle I hade from the Colo. Bought from Mr. Porter 2 hanks brown silk at 1/3 to my Accott. with him. Bought from Mr. John Glassel 1 Yd. black Ribbon for my hair at 1/ and 2 Yds. figgur'd Do. at 1/ per yd. to give Nancy Beck for Altering 2 vestcoats for me, my Pocket expence this day 1/¾ Cury. Recd. from Mr. Fultoun[106] Taylor In Toun ⅜ Yd Buckram in a present.

SUNDAY 25TH.

Before and after Dinner on board the Betsy Schooner with Mr. Foster Chief Mate of her who is now on his Voyage to the West Indies, & is to give me a call at his return.

MUNDAY 26TH.

Nil.

TUESDAY 27TH.

Do.

WEDNESDAY 28TH.

Do.

[*Page 103d*]   ### THURSDAY 29TH. JUNE 1775.

Nil.

FREIDAY 30TH.

Do.

SATURDAY 1ST. JULY.

At noon I went to Frederickg. and bought 15 bigg Double Guilt buttons at 4/9, One hank silk twist at 1/ and one Ounce brown thread at 6d. my Pocket expence this day 1/. I returned home an houre before sun doun.

SUNDAY 2D.

At home all day.

MUNDAY 3D.

Nil.

TUESDAY 4TH.

Do.

WEDNESDY. 5TH.

Do.

THURSDAY 6TH.

Do.

FREIDAY 7TH.

This day at sunset Colo. Daingerfield finished cutting down 260 Bushels sowing of wheat in fifteen days with seven Cradlers and it was done in 6 days less time than 203 bushels sowing was last Harvest and with fewer hands. For this Harvest his money payments to Out labourers is reduced no less than £18. 4. 6d. lower than it was last and at same time the Wheat better put up all which is chiefly owing to the Activity of Anthony Frazer the present Overseer.

SATURDAY 8TH.

This mor[n]ing began to bring Wheat to the Barn with two Carts Six Oxen in the one, and three Horses in the Other.

[*Page104th*]   SUNDAY 9TH. JULY 1775.

Nil.

MUNDAY 10TH.

TUESDAY 11TH.

WEDNESDAY 12TH.

THURSDAY 13TH.

FREIDAY 14TH.

This evening I recd. my Brown Coat I brought to this Country with me new mounted and turned by One Kid: Beck a Taylor for doing of which I paid him six shillings as per Agreemt. before he began to [do?] it.

SATURDAY 15TH.

Nil.

SUNDAY 16.

This day I went to Church in Toun and heard sermon preached by one Mr. Murray his text was Math: 6th. & 24th. V. I was no pocket expence this day.

MUNDAY 17TH.

Nil.

TUESDAY 18TH.

Do.

WEDNESDAY 19.

This day I was Informed that Mrs. Daingerfield hade made a Complaint upon me to the Colo. for not waiting after Breackfast & dinner (some times) in order to take the Children along with me to Scholl; I imagine she has hade a grudge against me since the middle of Feby. last the reason was, that one night in the Nursery I wheep'd Billie for crying for nothing & she came in & carried him out from me. Some nights after he got into the same humour & his Papa The Colo. hearing him call'd me & Asked why I cou'd hear him do so & not corect him for it; Upon that I told him how Mrs. Daingerfield had behaved when I did corect him. At that he was angry with her.

[*Page 105th*]   THURSDAY 20TH. JULY 1775.

Nil.

FREIDAY 21ST.

Do.

SATURDAY 22D.

On Saturdy. 13 Inst. some words happned betwixt John McDearmand & the Colo. about John's not being expedecious enough About
stacking and requiring too many hands to attend him upon which
John left the work immedeatly and has not returned since. And by
the Accots. in my hands I find the Colo. is in Johns debt £9. 10. 9
Virga. Currancy.

SUNDAY 23D.

Mrs. Porter having been here all night from Toun; I this day after
breackfast brought all the boys with their books into the passage to
the Colo. who heard each of them read and was highly pleased with
their performance. Mrs. Porter likeways told that her sons did me
great honour; as well as the rest.

MUNDAY 24TH.

Nil.

TUESDAY 25TH.

Do.

WEDNESDY. 26TH.

This day at noon was finished the bringing hom and stacking the
Colos. Wheat haveing 18 Stacks of 100 Bushels each by Computation
besides a Large Barn fill'd up to the roof. It was brought home this
year in 15 days less time than it was last year. I this day ate water-
melon of my own planting it being the first I ate this Season.

THURSDAY 27TH.

Nil.

FREIDAY 28TH.

Do.

SATURDAY 29TH.

At Town this afternoon & dined in Mr. Porters & retd. at night.

[*Page 106th*]   SUNDAY 30TH. JULY 1775.

At home. This day I ate part of a water Melon of my own planting 2 feet 4 Inches round the one way & 1 foot 9 Ins. round the other way.

MUNDAY 31ST.

This morning I planted one hill with some of the seeds of the water Mellon I ate Yesterday.

TUESDY. AUGT. 1ST.

Nil.

WEDNESDAY 2D.

Yesterday the Colo. Began to Sow Wheat for the ensewing croop. This day came to School Wm. John. & Lucy Patties, and are to pay conform to the time they Attend. Expecting a Visit of Mr. Kenedy sent to Town for a bottle of Vest India Rum which cost me 1/3 Currancy.

THURSDAY 3D.

Nil.

FREIDAY 4TH.

Do.

SATURDAY 5TH.

Do.

SUNDAY 6TH.

Do.

MUNDAY 7TH.

Do.

TUESDAY 8TH.

Do.

WEDNESDAY 9TH.

Do.

THURSDAY 10TH.

Do.

FREIDAY 11TH.

Do.

SATURDAY 12TH.

Do.

SUNDAY 13TH.

Do.

MUNDAY 14TH.

Do.

[*Page 107th*]   TUESDAY 15TH. AUGUST 1775.

WEDNESDAY 16TH.

Last night I seed the Anthony Man of War & the Lucy Friggat at Belvidera closs engaged Yard Arm & Yard Arm, upon which I steered my course for Blanket bay within School Cape if afterwds. they boarded each other let time give Information of the same; This being the 2d. Engagemt. that's happed lately.

THURSDAY 17TH.

Nil.

FREIDAY 18TH.

Do.

SATURDAY 19

Do.

SUNDAY 20TH.

Do.

MUNDAY 21ST.

Do.

TUESDAY 22D.

This morning the Colo. began to trade out wheat in the Yard with horses which is done in the following manner Vizt. They take wheat from the Stack & spreads it about eight foot broad in a large circle and with as many horses as they have, they ride upon it round & round & 3 or 4 men keep always turning & stirring it up, & by this method they with 10 or 12 horses will trade out 100 Bushels in a day. Where they trade Just now is 300 feet Circumference.

WEDNESDAY 23D.

Nil.

THURSDAY 24TH.

Do.

Freiday 25th.

This evening Edwin Daingerfield Cut One of his temples to the bone by a fall from a grape vine, I not being with him, but was the first that found him under the bank where it happned.

Saturday 26th.

Nil.

Sunday 27

Do.

[*Page 108th*]   Munday 28th. Augt. 1775.

Coppy of my 4th. Letter wrote this day to my wife.

My Dearest Life

Your most agreeable favours I recd. 27th. May last, which was dated 1st. March, And you may belive me it gave me the greatest satisfaction I have hade for twelve months past to hear from your own hand that you my Dearest Jewell and my sweet Infants are & has been in a good state of health since I left you, As I still am & has been for the above time, For which we have all great reason to render all due praise to that ever Glorious Being who wisely governs & directs all our Acctions; And may he for the sake of him who suffered on the Cross for all sinners continoue to protect and direct you & all that conserns us for the better. I would have wrote you sooner after the recept of yours, had I not been waiting an Answer to a verry long letter I wrote 6th. Decr. last which I find hade not come to your hand when you wrote me but am hopefull it has long before now & an Answer to it on its way here. When you write me I intreat you to do it on a sheet of the largest post paper you can get & leave no waste room in it, as the postage is no more than if it was three lines on ¼ sheet. And sure I am you can find subject enough to fill a sheet of paper as you well know that whatever comes from your hand must be agreeable. I am extreamly glade to hear you are Chiefly directed by your Brothr. Capt. Craigie and I think myself highly obliged to him both for his advice and assistance to you in my absence, I having of this date wrote him myself and given him my most hearty thanks for his good offices to you and begged his continouance of the same.

I begg you to advise with your Brother on that paragraph of my last letter with respect to your moving here, & I have likeways now begged him to write me his thoughts on the same subject, so that I expect you will both write me fully on recept of this, [*Page 109*] and I begg you to put him in mind of it. I have also wrote him to be assisting to you, untill such time as the ports are oppen for trade betwixt Britain and the Collonies & the disputes made up betwixt them, for untill that is done there is no such thing as remitting money or goods from any part of America to Britain, which gives me a good deall of trouble on your Accott. of which your Brothr. can more fully inform you of, As also of the engagements that has been betwixt the British troops and the forces of the united Collonies before Boston as room wou'd faill me here to do it. As to Mr. Forbes pray make my Compts. to him & spouse and tell him from me that I make no doubt from the Information I have of his making good bread in this Country for that a Journaman Bricklayer here has no less than five shillings a day Currancy which is equall to four shillings Str. And I am aquanted with an Undertaker in that branch of bussiness who is now set down on good Estate and rides in his Chair every day. But if he was to come over he must resolve to give closs application to bussiness & keep from drinking. About 7 months ago a Gentleman in Fredericksbg. hade his two sons taken from the high school there and put under my care for which he pays me £5 a year. He is an English man himself and his Lady from Edinburgh,[107] & I have the pleasure to have given the parents such satisfaction that I hade sent me in a present two silk vestcoats and two pair of britches ready to put on for changes in summer. I observe my Dear Dogg George writes me his name at the foot of your letter, But I am surprized that you take no notice of Jack & Bettie. But I hope you will not faill to be more particular about them in your next, and give my blessing to them all and tell them from me that I hope they will be obedient to you in every respect & mind their books. Before I get things brought to a bearing was any vessell by chance to put into Bressaysound bound for any part of Virginia or for Powtomack river which divides

this Collony from Maryland, I wou'd have you at all events make
your [*Page 110*] Brother apply for your Passage with the Childreen and a servant and imediatly dispose of every article in the
house your Feather Bedds Bedding & Cloaths excepted, and if
any money to spare lay it out in Linen; and write me imediatly
on your Aravell here by post and I shou'd soon be with you.
(May God grant that such a cast may happen to you). I must
now conclude by offering my Compts. to Mr. & Mrs. Vance, and
all who enquires for me in a friendly way, with my blessing to
you my sweet life and my Dear Infants is all at present from, My
Dearest Jewell, your ever Affectionate Husband while—Signed
J. Hr.

Belvidera 28th. Augt. 1775.

Addressed to Mrs. John Harrower in Lerwick, Zetland, by
Edinburgh, North Britain.

Same date   A Coppy
Dr. Sir

I make no doubt but by my not laying my mind oppen to you
sooner I have partly incur'd your displeasure, But before I am
done shall hope for your excusing me, And allow me to take this
opportunity of returning you my most gratefull Acknowledge-
ments for your good advice & Assistance to my Dearest Wife &
Childreen since we have been absent from one another, and I
earnestly intreat your continouance of the same and am hopefull
you will not see her in strait untill I am able to repay you, and
wherin I can serve you or yours it shall never be wanting on my
part. My design of leaving Zetland for some time was only
known to my wife; And the making it known to any person else
wou'd not in all probabilytie wou'd not have hindred it; I being
so straitned that nothing but money upon Intrest for some Considerable time cou'd have saved me from being personally exposed; But when I left the Country, I did not intend going further than Holland, or even London cou'd I have found bussiness
there to my likeing but not finding that, and the frost being
strong in Holland, I was determined to see what I cou'd do in
this Western World. And as to [*Page 111*] my bussiness and Situation here, Annie can fully inform you if she has not already
done it. Here I have keept my health much better than ever I did

before in any place, and am as happily situated as I cou'd wish hade I my wife and Childreen with me, Only not in a way at present to make much money, tho I hope in a short time I shall be able to make more; I have now wrote Annie to advise with you, with respect to her moving to this Country with the Childreen, and shall expect her thoughts upon it in her next; And I earnestly begg of you that on receipt of this you take the trouble to write me yourself & give me your mind on the same subject, likeways let me know how trade goes with any thing else that is remarcable in the country, And Annie will give you the proper directions for me.

Untill the disputes betwixt Government and the Collonies are settled there is no such thing as getting any remittance made to any part in Britain; Hostilities being already begun at Boston and three Engagements already fought betwixt the British troops and the provincialls the last of which on the 17th. June last at Charleston near Boston, when the Provincialls gaind the day as they did of the other two. In this last Engt. Genll. Gage hade above a thousand men left dead on the field of Battle & 500 wounded. Among the dead are many of the British officers, which is owing to the Americans takeing sight when they fire, An instance of which I shall here give you. Colo. Washington of this Collony being appointed Generalissimo of all the American Forces raised & to be raised, made a demand of 500 Rifflemen from the frontiers of this Colly. But those that insisted on going far exceeded the number wanted when in order to avoid giving offence, The commanding officer chuse his Compty. by the following method Vizt. He took a board of a foot squar and with Chalk drew the shape of a moderate nose in the center and nailed it up to a tree at 150 yds. distance and those who came nighest the mark with a single ball was to go. But by the first 40 or 50 that fired the nose was all blown [*Page 112th*] out of the board, and by the time his Compy. was up the board shared the same fate. How or when these differences will [end?] God only knows, But the Americans are determined to stand by one another to the last man and all export & import are intirely stopt also planting of Tobacco. On 26th. last Mo. wheat Harvest was finised on this Plantation by getting the last of it brought home & stacked, the Amount of which will be about 3 thousand bushells, and now ten ploughs are at work every day ploughing wheat into the ground again for the next croop. It is sown here in the same field where the Indian corn is growing, so that both grow together untill the Mo. of Novr. when the corn is gathered and the field cleared of the stalks. Indian corn is planted at six feet distance each way as streight and regular as you do Cabbage in a garden and when it is sprung up only two stalks left in a hill; It will grow from five to twelve or fourteen [feet?] high & each stalk will have two if not three Ears on it, and each Ear will have from five to Eight hundred grains on it the size of which you know. But from Apll. the time it is planted untill now that the Wheat is sown among it, It is keept as clean of grass & weeds as a garden by the Ploughs running continually betwixt the rows first the one way and then the other, and the Howers going round the hills with their hows, and without this work it wou'd come to no perfection. Of Corn there will be on this Plantation about 8 or 9 Hundred Barrells at five Bushells to the Barrell, about 350 Barrell will be used for the Nigers and Horses, the rest for sale, the price about 10/ per Barrell. As for what the White ates of it is but triffling for three Barrell of Corn is rather more than any one Man can use in a year let him ate no other bread, the value of which is only 30/. All the white people on the Plantation is the Colo. his Lady, five Childreen, a Housekeeper an Overseer and myself, But I think no more now of seeing 40 or 50 Nigers every day, than I did of seeing so many Dabling wifes at Johnsmiss[108] with [*Page 113th*] single Stockins, two or three M of the best of which if I hade here I cou'd sell to Good Accott. On casting my Eye out of the window I cannot help most heartily wishing you hade some of the most Charming Watermellons I have now growing and some of them ripe within less than 3 Yds. of where I sitt. Some of which will weigh from 20 to 30 lb. My Plantation for my Amusement consists of the following Articles Vizt. Water melons, Mush-melons, Cucumbers, Pumpkins, Gourds Spanish Pitatoes and Cotton. So much for Plantation information.

I am truely affraid I have incroached on your patience already in giving you the trouble of reading this long epistle therefore I shall conclude at this time by earnestly entreating you to write me at Large and let me know your thoughts on the present disputes betwixt the Collonies and the Ministry. My Compts. to Mrs. Craigie Miss Peggy & your two sons[109] to Mr. & Mrs.

Sands[110] and their Childreen and please Accept of the same your-self from him who is with sinceer regaird Dr. Sr. your Most Affte. Brothr. & Hul. Servt. J. Hr.

Belvidera 20th. August 1775. Addressed to Capt. James Craigie in Lerwick, Zetland, by Edinburgh, North Britain.

TUESDAY 29TH.

Nil.

WEDNESDAY 30TH.

Do.

THURSDAY 31ST.

Do.

FREIDAY SEPTR. 1ST.

Do.

SATURDAY 2D.

At noon rode to Town and delivered two letters to Mr. Henry Mitchell,[111] one for my wife & one for her Brother Capt. James Craigie After which I returd. home by Sundoun; At which time came on one of the hardest gales of wind & rain I have seen since I have been in the Country. It has tore many trees & brocke doun a deall of Corn & Tore all the Fodder to Pieces.

[*Page 114th*]   SUNDAY 3D. SEPTR. 1775.

At home all day.

MUNDAY 4TH.

Nil.

TUESDAY 5TH.

This morning Miss Lucy Gaines went up the Country to the Wilderness with her Brother who come for her to see her Mother who was sick.

WEDNESDAY 6TH.

This day I was informed by Mr. Frazer That Mrs. Daingerfield talking to him of me that morning about some Glue disresptfully call'd me Old Harrower by which and her behaveiour to myself I find her grudge continous tho she has not courage to say any thing to myself well knowing she has [no] foundation to go upon.

THURSDAY 7TH.

Nil.

FREIDAY 8TH.

Do.

SATURDAY 9TH.

Do.

SUNDAY 10TH.

This day came Dick a Servt. belonging to Mr. Anderson from Toun & a Comerade of his to see me & Brought me a pair new shoes & a pair for Mr. Frazer also a Bottle Vest India Rum which we drank in School in Company with Mr. Frazer.

MUNDAY 11TH.

This day sent my letter to wife to Fredericksbg. by Mr. Frazer & gave him 1/6 to give with it at the post office as Postage to New York. But Mr. Brown my friend the Clark told Mr. Frazer he wou'd send it home free for me by a Ship going to saile.

TUESDAY 12TH.

Nil.

WEDNESDAY 13TH.

Do.

THURSDAY 14TH.

Do.

[*Page 115th*]   FREIDAY 15TH. SEPT. 1775.

Wrote my [wife] The 5th. Letter this day from Virginia, This being the Coppy.

My Dearest Life

Yours of the 12th. May last I received 2d. Inst. imediatly after sending off one for you & one for your Afftt. brother dated 28th. last Mo. Both which will come to your Hand I imagine at the same time that this will as I am obligded to send this to New York by post in order to come to London by the Pacquet, There being no more Opportunities from this Collony to Glasgow this season, by reason that the Nonimportation & Nonexportation Acts of the Continental Congress now takes place and will continue untill the disputes betwixt Great Britain and the Colonys be settled.

And I intreat you imediatly on receipt of this letter to wait on your Brother and show it to him, and he will more fully inform you of these Matters than room will permit me to do here, As my principal Design of writing you this so soon after my last is to make you as easy as possible I can both with respect to my not sending for you and making you a remittance. As to the first of these I cou'd not be certain if you wou'd come to this Country or not untill I recd. your last letter. But as I find by it you are satisfied to come here, you may belive me nothing in this world can give me equall satisfaction to my having you & my Dr. Infants with me. As a proof of which I have ever signiefied the same in my letter to your brother. And I now declare unto you as I sinceerly write from my heart before God, that I will how soon I am able point out the way to you how you may get here, And at same time make you what remittance I can in order to Assist you on your way. But you must [*Page 116*] consider that as I hade not a shilling in my pocket when I left you It must take me some time befor I can be able to make you a remittance. Therefore I even pray you for Gods sake to have patience and keep up your heart and no means let that fail you: For be ashured the time is not Longer to you than me, And the National disputes & the stopage of trade betwixt this and the Mother Country if not soon settled will of course make the time longer as your brother will inform you. As to your Jocks upon me with respect to my getting a Virginian Lady it is the least in all my thoughts and am determined to leave that Jobb for you by aiding your sons with your advice to them in their choise of wifes among the Virginian Ladys; For I am resolved (as at first) to do as much for you as God is pleased to put in my power.

I am glade you are moved to a place of the Town,[112] as you say agreeable to your own disposition, but an extreamly fearfull for you on Accott. of the earthen floor: And considering Forbes behavour to you, what I wrote you in my last conserning him you have prudence enough to keep it to yourself, and I will give myself no further trouble here about him. I am verry uneasy about your being so tender this Spring But am hopefull you have quite got the better of it before now. At same time it gives me great satisfaction to hear the Childreen are all well, and that Jock is still at Walls.[113] I hope he is now making some progress in his Education, and am hopefull George will do the same. As for

Betts Im not affraid of her considering whose hands she is under. I have nothing further to add at present only I again begg of you to keep a good heart and do the best you can untill it please God to enable me to assist you & for aught I think you shall hear no more from me untill [*Page 117*] I be able to remitt you either more or less.

My Compliments and sinceer good wishes to your Brother Mr. Craigie, his spouse & Family likeways my Compts. to Mr. & Mrs. Vance, and all others wh[o] may enquire for me in a freendly way; with my sinceer love and prayers to God for you my Dearest Jewell & Childreen is all at present from your ever Afftt. Husbd. Signed J. H. Belvidera 15th. Septr. 1775.
Adressed To Mrs. John Harrower in Lerwick Zetland by the New York Packet to London & by Edinr. North Britain.

SATURDAY 16TH.

This afternoon I got plenty of Grapes which grows in many places in the woods from the 1st. Inst untill now being the time of them.

SUNDAY 17TH.

At home all day.

MUNDAY 18TH.

Nil.

TUESDAY 19TH.

Do.

WEDNESDAY 20TH.

Do.

THURSDAY 21ST.

Do.

FREIDAY 22D.

Do.

SATURDAY 23D.

At sun doun returned Miss Lucy Gaines from the Wilderness her Mother having been sick.

SUNDAY 24TH.

This day after dinner Miss Lucy put into my hands for my perusal a love letter she recd. while she was up the Country from a young man worth an Estate of £400. She hade not seen or heard from him for three Years befor. She says she does & always did hate him. As it is a curiosity I shall here insert it Verbatum and Just as it is adressed & spelled. [*Page 118*]

> my deear love and the delite of my life very well remembur the great sattisfaction we have had in Each others Company but now is grone Stranger to Each other I understand you are a going to be marrid and I wish you a good husband with all my hart if you are ingaigd and if not I shuld think my self happy in making you mistress of my hart and of Evrething Els as I am worth if you culd have as much good will for me as I have for you we might live I belive very happy you may depend on my Cincerety If you think fit to Except of my offer I will make you my lawfull wife as sone as posoble if not I hope no harme don tho I can nevor forgit your preshus lips as I have Cist so offten and am very desiours to make them my one my Cind love and best respct to you my dove; this from your poor but faithfull lover till death PS pray let me no by the barer wheathar it is worth my while to put mysilf to the truble to com & see you or not
> Aadressed To Mrs. Lewse Gains

MUNDAY 25TH.

Nil.

TUESDAY 26TH.

Do.

WEDNESDAY 27TH.

Do.

THURSDAY 28

This morning I recd. from Benjamin Edge by the hand of his daughter two Dollars, one half, & one Quarter Dollar being in all sixteen shillings and Six pence in part payment for teaching his son & daughter. Same day I seed a Compy. of 70 Men belonging to one of the Regiments of Regullars now raised here for the defence of the rights & liberties of this Colly. in particular & of North America in Generall. They were on their March to Williamsburg.

FREIDAY 29TH.

Bassets Birth day.

[Page 119th]   SATURDAY 30TH. SEPTR. 1775.

Nil.

SUNDAY 1ST.

Octr. at home all day.

MUNDAY 2D.

Nil.

TUESDAY 3D.

Mrs. Daingerfield returd. home.

WEDNESDAY 4TH.

Hard rain.

THURSDAY 5TH.

Do.

FREIDAY 6TH.

Do.

SATTURDAY 7TH.

Do.

SUNDAY 8TH.

Excessive hard rain all day.

MUNDAY 9TH.

Billie Porter taken sick.

TUESDAY 10TH.

Billie Do. at home.

WEDNESDAY 11TH.

Billie went to Town with his Mama.

THURSDAY 12TH.

Company here last night Vizt. Old Mrs. Waller, her son and his wife[114] and at school there Mr. Heely Schoolmaster & Mr. Brooks Carpenter and they with Mr. Frazer & myself played whist and danced untill 12 oClock, Mr. Heely playing the Fidle & dancing. We drank one bottle of rum in time. Mr. Frazer verry sick after they went home.

Yesterday came here Mary Fitsgyls to spin flax. She is an Irish girle and has now been Nine year in Virginia. She is still unmarried but has had a Child to one Dolton[115] a Taylor in Fredricksg. The boy is with her & is now two years old.

FREIDAY 13TH.

Billie Daingerfields birth day.

SATURDAY 14TH.

At Saml. Edge's for money.

SUNDAY 15TH.

I was all ready to go to Mount Church in Compy. with Mr. Frazer & Miss Lucy but Miss Lucy not getting a saddle put a stop to us all.

After dinner we all three walked as far as Mr. Becks & in our Absence came Mr. Kennedy from Town to see me and on Missing me left a letter for me from Mr. Payne Schoolmr.[116]

[*Page 120th*]   MUNDAY 16TH. OCTR. 1775.

This morning 3 Men went to work to break, swingle and heckle flax and one woman to spin in order to make coarse linnen for Shirts to the Nigers, This being the first of the kind that was made on the plantation. And before this year there has been little or no linnen made in the Colony.

TUESDAY 17TH.

Two women spining wool on the bigg wheel and one woman spinning flax on the little wheel all designed for the Nigers.

WEDNESDAY 18TH.

Nil.

THURSDAY 19TH.

Do.

FREIDAY 20TH.

Do.

SATURDAY 21ST.

This morning Mr. Frazer pull'd up & brought me from the field one grain of wheat which hade 21 Branches the longest of which was 3 feet 2 Inches and the thickest was ¾ s. of an inch in circumference and the Broadest of the Blades was ⅛ s. of an inch. This evening came here Mr. Heely Schoolmr. and Thos. Brooks Carpenter to see me & stayed all night. Mr. Frazer at his Mothers.

SUNDAY 22D.

This morning Mr. Heely and Mr. Brooks went home and put on clean linnen and then returned & dined with Miss Lucy & me & then spent the afternon verry agreeably; At night Mr. Frazer returned.

MUNDAY 23D.

One Freiday last I lent to Miss Lucy one pair of my Shoes to spin with. This day General Washingtons Lady dined here, As did her son and Daugr. in Law, Mrs. Spotswood, Mrs. Campbell, Mrs. Dansie, Miss Washington & Miss Dandrige,[117] They being all of the highes Rank & fortunes of any in this Colony.

[*Page 121st*]   TUESDAY 24TH. OCTR. 1775.

Nil.

WEDNESDAY 25TH.

Do.

THURSDAY 26TH.

Do.

FREIDAY 27TH.

Do.

SATURDAY 28TH.

Last night came here to school Mr. Heely & Thos. Brooks in order to spend the evening, but by reason of Mr. Frazer's not coming from the House, & some stories told them by Mrs. Richards in order to sow disention; She being realy a Wolf cloathed with a lambs skin & the greatest Mischief maker I have seen in all my Travels. The first time I seed her, I cou'd observe in her countenance Slyness & deceet, & I have always avoided going to the House as much as possible, But now I realy think she ought to be avoided by every christian who regairds peace and their own character. They both went home at 10 pm.

Sunday 29th.

Yesterday at noon Mr. Heely came here and asked me to take a walk with him in order to see Miss Molly White[118] late housekeeper at Newpost she having some shirts of his making for him, and after crossing the river we found her at an Aunts house of hers one Mrs. Hansfords where we stayed all night, and this day Miss Molly came with us two Miles to a Gentlemans house in our way home, & after aquanting Mr. Heely where his shirts was ready for him the conversation turned upon clearing themselves to each other of most malicious stories raised by the above Mrs. Richards in order to set them at variance & included with them was Miss Lucy Gaines our housekeeper, & myself. But now that every one has discovered the Snake, I belive in time coming her bite will be avoided.

Munday 30th.

The House Clock cleaned. And John McDearmen Warped 21 Yds. cloth for the Nigers.

Tuesday 31st.

I Eate the first new bread this year.

[*Page 122d*]   Wednesday 1st. Novr. 1775.

Nil.

Thursday 2d.

Do.

Freiday 3d.

Do.

SATURDAY 4.

Last night Mr. Frazer & me Went to Snow creek to see John Mc-Dearman but on our Araviel there we found his wife in Labour, so imediatly returned home and Aquanted Miss Lucy who went back with us to her assistance, And about One this morning she was delivered of a son; So we all stayed there untill day light this morning. (Saturday I mean).

SUNDAY 5TH.

At home untill after Dinner when I went to Snow creek with Miss Lucy, and we come home at sun setting. A deall of Company here to day.

MUNDAY 6TH.

Nil. Suckie[119] Delivd. of a son who is baptised George.

TUESDAY 7TH.

Do.

WEDNESDAY 8TH.

Do.

THURSDAY 9TH.

Upon Thursday 2d. Inst. there was a Camp Marked out close at the back of the school for a Batalion of 500 private men besides officers and they imediatly began to erect tents for the same. And this day the whole was finished for 250 men being 50 tents for the privates & 6 Do. for officers & 3 Do. for the Comissary & his Stores, with one for a Buffalo which is to be shown which I shall afterwards describe.—This day the 250 men being 5 Companys from different parts aravied at the Camp the other 5 Companys not being as yet compleated.[120]

FREIDAY 10TH.

All the men encampt. And I Decampt from the Nursery by Mrs. Ds. order.

[*Page 123d*]   SATURDAY 11TH. NOVR. 1775.

At 11 OClock forenoon I rode to Toun & bought one stone Mugg & Tin pot at 10d. & 1¼ Yd. Linen at 5/ of which I want two stocks for winter wear, & the rest of it I made a present to Miss Lucy for her readdyness to do any little thing for me; I seed no worsted stockins for sale but one pair all Moth eaten & as they were they asked no less than 6/ for them. I dined at Mr. Porters Spent 7½ at Mr. Anderson & then came home by sun doun.

SUNDAY 12TH.

This day a great number of Company from Toun & Country to see the Camp four of which (Gentlemen) paid me a visite which put me to 1/3 expense for a bottle of rum. At noon by Accident one of the Captains tents was set on fire & all consumed but none of things of any Accott. Lost.

MUNDAY 13TH.

This forenoon the Coll. sent a Waggon Load of Turnups & Pitatoes to the Camp as a present for all the men.

TUESDAY 14TH.

All the minute-men in the Camp employed learning their exercise.

WEDNESDAY 15TH.

This morning I drank a small dram of rum made thick with brown suggar for the cold, it being the first dram I have drunk since I lived on the Plantation.

THURSDAY 16TH.

The soldiers at Muster.

FREIDAY 17TH.

The soldiers at Do., and I left of[f] going into the Nurserry & taking charge of the childreen out of school.

[Page *124th*]   SATURDY 18TH. NOVR. 1775.

Nil.

SUNDAY 19TH.

Do.

MUNDAY 20TH.

Do.

TUESDAY 21ST.

Do.

WEDNESDAY 22D.

Do.

Thursday 23d.

Do.

Freiday 24th.

Do.

Saturday 25th.

Do.

Sunday 26.

Numbers of Company at the camp.

Munday 27th.

Do.

Tuesday 28th.

Do.

Wednesday 29.

This day the camp was brocke up and the whole Batallion dismissed after each private receiving 22 days pay at 1/4 per day & 1/ for provisions out & home. During the time the camp was by the school it cost me 8/1½ of expences which is more by 2/ than it cost me for 12 Months before.

Thursday 30th.

Nil.

Freiday 1st. Decemr.

Do.

Saturday 2d.

At noon went to Toun and seed two Companys of regulars from the Ohio among which was one real Indian. He was of a Yelow couler

short brod faced & rather flat nosed, and long course black [hair?]
quite streight. He spoke verry good english. I staid in Toun all night
& sleept at Mr. Andersons; I bought from Mr. Porter a black Silk
Handkerchief at 5/.

SUNDAY 3D.

After breackfast I went & found out Miss Molly White & left with
her cloth to make me two winter Stocks & a Stock to make them by.
Dined in Toun, came home in the afternoon.

[*Page 125th*]   MUNDAY 4TH. DECEMR. 1775.

Nil.

TUESDAY 5TH.

Do.

WEDNESDAY 6TH.

Left home this day 2 Years.

THURSDAY 7TH.

Nil.

FREIDAY 8TH.

At night the Coll. came home from Toun having been there with
Mrs. Daingerfield, their Daugr. & youngest son since Tuesday last,
disposing of the returns of a Niger fellow sent to the Vest Indies for
the practice of running away; The returns for him in rum and Suggar
Amounted to £60 Virga. Cury. Anthy. with Lucy the three nights
past.

SATURDAY 9TH.

Mrs. Daingerfield & the two Childn. returned home also the Niger
wench, who waited on them.

SUNDAY 10TH.

At noon I went to Benjamin Edge's and staid dinner when he gave

me two dollars in part paymt. of his Chi[l]dreens education, the afternoon excessive rany.

MUNDAY 11TH.

Nil.

TUESDAY 12TH.

Do.

WEDNESDAY 13TH.

At noon the Coll. set off for his Quarter at Chickahomany in order
to recive money.

THURSDAY 14TH.

FREIDAY 15TH.

SATURDAY 16TH.

SUNDAY 17TH.

At home all day.

MUNDAY 18TH.

This morning before day light I found the Anthony, Man of War
& the Lucy Friggat of this Place both Moor'd head & stern along side
of each other in Blanket Bay within school cape, this being the second
time they have been Moored in the same harbour. Novr. 11th. being
the first time.

TUESDAY 19TH.

Nil.

WEDNESDAY 20TH.

Do.

THURSDAY 21ST.

Jas. & Billie Porter left school.

FREIDAY 22D.

A great fall of snow.

[*Page 126th*]   SATURDAY 23D. DECEMR. 1775.

Nil.

SUNDAY 24TH.

Do.

MUNDAY 25.

Last night the Coll. returd. home but says he recd. no Cash for out of odds £100 he did not git one Shilling. At night D - - - k.

TUESDAY 26TH.

Sick all day, at night Do.

WEDNESDAY 27TH.

1st   Both the last nights quite drunk was I,
         Pray God forgive me [of] the sin;
      But had I been in good company,
         Me in that case No man had seen.

2d   Plac'd by myself, without the camp,
         As if I were unclean;
      No freendly soul, does my floor tramp,
         My greiff to ease, or hear my moan.

3d.   For in a prison at large I'm plac't,
         Boun'd to it, day and night;
      O, grant me patience, God of grace,
         And in thy paths make me walk right.

4th   This day alone, at home I am,
         Repenting sadly and full sore

That ever the like, unto me came.

When this I see, The cause I will repent for ever more.

THURSDAY 28TH.

This morning sett off at 8 AM on foot for Toun & when I was a Mile from it was obliged to strip off shoes and stockings & wade, in order to my safe crossing a run.[121] I dined at Mr. Porters & was there till after 3 pm, Then went to Mr. Andersons where I stayed all night and spent the evening as sober as a Judge.

FREIDAY 29TH.

Came home to Dinner.

SATURDAY 30TH. & SUNDAY 31ST.

At home. Nil.

[*Page 127th*]   MUNDAY 1ST. JANY. 1776.

Last night came home Mr. Frazer after being eight days absent and after dark. The black Tender Barnabie came to School with orders from the Colonel in Petticoats alias the Lucy Frigget, For the Anthony man of War to attend her imediatly at, or within Cape Kitchen, from thence they Steered for Nursery Harbour within great Bay; where they both came to an Anchor untill after 10 pm when the Anthony u[n]moored & sailed for Sch. cape.

TUESDAY 2D.

Dined in the Nursery by order.

WEDNESDAY 3D.

Mrs. Porter & Jezebel here.

THURSDAY 4TH.

This morning the whole wheat in the Barn was found to be hot & some of it begun to Sprout upon which it was all run throug the fans & out [of] 1250 Bushels there was about 65 Bushels lost which is owing to a small insect called Weavle which breeds in the grain eats all the inside out & then comes out itself and flies away. Jezebel here all night.

FREIDAY 5TH.

Nil.

SATURDAY 6TH.

Do.

SUNDAY 7TH.

Went to Church on foot and heard Mr. Maree preach his Text was in the 5 Chapr. of the 1st. Epistle Genl. of John & the 3d. verse.

MUNDAY 8TH.

TUESDAY 9TH.

WEDNESDAY 10TH.

This day we hade the Confirmation of Norfolk being reduced to ashes by the Men of War & British Troops under Command of Lord Dunmore. It was the Largest Toun in the Collony and a place of great Trade, it being situate a little within the Capes. Severall Women & Childn. are killed.

[*Page 128th*]   THURSDAY 11TH. JANY. 1776.

Nil.

FREIDAY 12TH.

Do.

SATURDAY 13TH.

After 12 O Clock I went six Miles into the Forrest to one Daniel Dempsies[122] to see if they woud spin three pound of Cotton to run 8 yds. per lb., 2/3ds. of it belonging to Miss Lucy Gaines for a goun & 1/3d. belonging to myself for Vestcoats, which they agreed to do if I carried the cotton there on Saturdy. 27th. Inst.

SUNDAY 14TH.

At 11 AM I sett out for Mansfield the seat of Man Page Esqr. in order to see one Mr. Reid[123] Gaerdner who came from Dunkell in Scotland. Mr. Scott[124] Watch maker from Toun being also with him I staid with them untill after sun doun, having dined & being very genteely entertained. Mr. & Mrs. Porter & all their Childreen came here to dinner and staid all night.

MUNDAY 15TH.

Miss Lucy spinning my croop of Cotton at night after her work is done to make me a pair gloves.

TUESDAY 16TH.

Nil.

WEDNESDAY 17TH.

This evening Miss Lucy came to School with Mr. Frazer & me, and finised my croop of Cotton by winding it, after its being dowbled & twisted the whole consisting of two ounces.

Thursday 18th.

Nil.

Freiday 19th.

This evening an express came for Mr. Frazer from his Mother[125] for him to come and see one of his Brothers who was greatly brused by a tree falling on him upon Wednesday last in the new ground where the Negroes were clearing.

Saturday 20th.

At home all day.

Sunday 21st.

Went to Church & heard Mr. Maryee preach, his text was in the 8 Chap: of St. Mark & 38th. Verse. I dined in Town & retd. in the evening.

Munday 22d.

Mr. Frazer returd. last night.

[*Page 129th*]   Tuesday 23d. Jany. 1776.

This day I entred Edwin into the Latin Gramer.

Wednesdy. 24th.

Nil.

Thursday 25th.

Do.

Freiday 26th.

Do.

Saturday 27th.

After 12 pm I went to the forrest to the house of Daniel Dempsies and carried with me three pound of pick't Cotton two of which be-

longs to Miss Lucy Gaines and one to me, which his wife has agreed
to spin to run 8 Yds. per lb., I paing her five shillings per lb. for spinning it and it is to be done by the end of May next.

SUNDAY 28TH.

At home, Hard frost with Snow.

MUNDAY 29TH.

Nil.

TUESDAY 30TH.

This evening Miss Lucy Gaines came to school, and put up with
Suggar a Quart mugg full of Pasimmons to preserve them; & after
staying untill 11 pm returned to the great house.

WEDNESDAY 31ST.

Nil.

THURSDAY 1ST. FEBY.

Do.

FREIDAY 2D.

Do.

SATURDAY 3D.

Do.

SUNDAY 4TH.

At home all day, Compy. at dinner. In the Afternoon aravied at his
seat at Newpost Major Spotswood[126] from the Army at Norfolk after
an absence of above 3 Mo. Last night John Robertson[127] Brothr. in
Law to Miss Lucy came here from the Wilderness to see her, &
Lodged with me in the school all night. In the evening Mr. Frazer returd. from his Mothrs. & his brothr. John[128] with him who brought
me some Tobacco for Snuff.

MUNDAY 5TH.

This day Anthony Frazer swapped his Bay Colt with his Brothr. John for his Sorrel Mare with foal and £12. 10/ to boot.

[*Page 130th*]   TUESDAY 6TH. FEBY. 1776.

Finished getting corn.

WEDNESDAY 7TH.

Nil.

THURSDAY 8TH.

Do.

FREIDAY 9TH.

On Sunday night last there appeared a dryness 'twixt the Anthony Man of War and the Lucy Friggat of this place, But it is now all over again; And this day she has told me freely about their Courtship, and that they design to be Married next fall, & that it was her own falt they were not married last fall; Upon which I told her she was to blame, & might perhaps have cause to repent putting it off so long & advised her to shorten the time if possible she could, which she aggreed to do upon me giving her verry good reasons for it.

SATURDAY 10TH.

This afternoon I went to Town and Bought a Ridding Saddle at £1. 7. 6 for which I gave an order on Mr. Porter for the money at same time recd. from Mr. Porter 10/ Cash. Bought one Briddle at 7/ from Mr. Jervis[129] & recd. in Cash from him 3/, Being 10/ in part paytt. of an order I hade on him for 20/. Bought one Ozt. Indigo at 1/3d and 1½ lb. hard soap at 1/6 & staid in Town all night. L. G. moord within School cape all night.

SUNDAY 11TH.

Returd. home by Midday.

MUNDAY 12TH.

Nil.

TUESDAY 13TH.

Do.

WEDNESDAY 14TH.

Do.

THURSDAY 15.

Do.

FREIDAY 16TH.

At night Delivered to Jno. McDearman 1 ½ lb. pickt Cotton at 1/6 per lb.

SATURDAY 17TH.

Mr. & Mrs. Daingerfield in Town all night.

SUNDAY 18.

Martin Heely here last night & this day.

MUNDAY 19TH.

Anthy. with Lucy all last night below.

TUESDAY 20TH.

Anthy. with Lucy all this night Do.

WEDNESDAY 21ST.

Lucy at school till late.

THURSDAY 22D.

Lucy at Do. Anthy. dry with her, But she over fond of him, which will turn to her disadvantage.

[*Page 131st*]   FREIDAY 23D. FEBY. 1776.

Lucy at school till late. Upon Munday 15 Jany. last Ganzera & Pattie went to John McDns. to spin wool & cotton for him & they continued with him until Tuesday 20th. Inst. being 31 work days in which time they spun 6 lb. of Wool & 8½ lb. Cotton to run nigh five yds. per lb.

SATURDAY 24TH.

At home all day.

SUNDAY 25TH.

At Mr. Beck's with Miss Lucy. In the evening Mr. Frazer returned from his Mothers & made me a present of a new Cotton Handkierchiff worth 2/ of his Mother's spinning & weaving & hemed for me by his sister.

After we went to Bed I tuched upon his marriage with Miss Lucy. He asked me if [I] thought it wou'd be a match, I told him I did; And asked him if he did not think so himself. He answered me that he had a great many thoughts, That he was young & cou'd hardly maintain himself, That it was a Daingerous situation & ought to be well considered off, That he hade a fickle Master to do with & was uncertain of his time here, That at any rate he was determined not to stay above another year here, if he staid that. I told him that one in his Bussiness cou'd afford to live better married, than a man in any Other Bussiness whatever, & that if he was married a great many articles might be made in his house at a verry small expence which run away with a deale of money from him when he went to the store. That every one who seed her (if they did her Justice) must allow her to be a genteel, cliver, weel looked girle & of a good temper, and that I wou'd be greatly decieved in her if she did not make an extream good wife. He allowed her to be a verry good Girle, But added that while he was single, if he was affronted he cou'd move at pleasure, which was not so easy done when married, for that after marriage soon came somethin else (meaning Childreen) which [*Page 132*] was not so easily removed, when perhaps one did not know where to go too when out of Bussiness. I told him as to that he cou'd never be at a loss haveing a good place of his own to go to when he pleased, upon which he dropped the subject. Upon the whole, I find he either does not chuse to own to me, that he designs to marrie her, or is as yet unsettled upon it if he will have her for his wife or not: And as matters seems to stand fair betwixt them at present I do not think it prudent to aquant Miss Lucy with this conversation at least for some time; As I wou'd willingly avoide every word that might give offence upon either side as I sinceerly think them well deserving of each other.

Munday 26th.

Mr. Frazer this night declared to me that he wou'd suffer to lose his right hand, if ever he had or ever wou'd mention it to any, That ever Miss Lucy was in School of an evening or any other time.

Tuesday 27th.

This day wrote Mr. Anderson and sent him by Abraham 3/ to buy me ½ Gallon of old spirits, but none being to be had for that money he sent me ½ Galn. of the best of Rum. At same time wrote Mr. Porter for two pound of brown suggar.

Wednesdy. 28th.

Recd. the 2 lb. brown suggar I wrote for.

Thursdy. 29.

Bott. 2 pair thd. stockins at 5/ per.

Freiday 1st. March.

Miss Lucy in School all last night, which fretted Mrs. Daingerfield this day, because she was Obliged to sleep in the Nursery with Johnnie. At noon I hade a conversation with Lucy, When she told me she had a mind never to come more nigh the School. I told her she ought not to breack off coming all at once, But to confine herself to the houre of 10 or 11 at farthest, And if he insisted on her staying longer to desire him to Marrie at once, & then they cou'd be at their full freedom. Same time I told her not to build too strongly on him as the time proposed to finish the Bargain was far distant, and he seemingly determined not to shorten it; Some time ago she asked him what answer he wou'd give me if I jested him on it. He answered, That he was courting Lucy & wou'd have her if he cou'd get her. Compare this with my conversation with Him 25th. Ulto.

[*Page 133d*]   SATURDAY 2D. MARCH 1776.

At Mr. Becks in the afternoon. In the evening John Frazer came here to see his brother. At night I made him a present of a pair pinchbk. shoe buckles in return for some Tobacco he sent me.

SUNDAY 3D.

Rode to Town Church in Coy. with A. Frazer, Jo. Frazer & Wm. Richards, heard Mr. Maryee Preach his text was in 1st. Tim: 4 Chapr. 8 Verse. At 9 AM Mr. & Mrs. Daingerfield set out for Port Royall. I returned home by 4 pm. This day I recd. a pair silver slive buttons with my name on them for some burred [?] lace I formerly gave to Brown the Silver Smith. The Anthy. Man of War obliged to unmoor from Blanket bay within school Cape & moor in Nurserry bay within Great house Cape.

MUNDAY 4TH.

Mr. & Mrs. Daingerfield not come home yet; Any. Man of War moored this night within great Howse cape.

TUESDAY 5TH.

This morning Bathurest Daingerfield got don reading through the Bible and the Newtestament, and began to learn to write 15 Ulto. I gave them Holyday this afternoon. Mr. & Mrs. Daingerfield not yet come home; The Any. Man of War moored this night also within great House cape.

WEDNESDAY 6TH.

A verry hard gale of wind last night. It blowed down one of the Brick Chimneys of Snow Creek Howse. At 4 pm Mr. & Mrs. Daingerfield came home from Portroyall, & Robt. Johnston[130] Mercht. in Coy. with them.

THURSDAY 7TH.

Nil.

FREIDAY 8TH.

Do.

SATURDAY 9TH.

Do.

SUNDAY 10TH.

This day I went to Benjn. Edge's & recd. 13/, It being the ballance due me for teachg. his two childreen. Anthy. Frazer went to bring home a Stallion Bott. by the Colo. at £100. Miss Lucy went to Church & to see her Mother who made her inraged against A. F. by telling her he had spoke disrespectfully of her, & heard others do so, without stopping them.

[*Page 134th*]   MUNDAY 11TH. MARCH 1776.

At night Mr. Frazer reeturnd with the Stallion Ariell,[131] colour all black. Same Night he satisfied Miss Lucy that all she had heard was false, So Matters twixt them continue on a fair footing.

TUESDAY 12TH.

Three hands began to cut wood for a house to the Stallion. It is building close by the School, Dementions 12 by 10.

WEDNESDY. 13.

Nil.

THURSDY. 14.

Do.

FREIDY. 15.

Do.

Saturdy. 16th.

Planted Cucumber, Musk, & Watter Melons, and One Hill with Guinea Musk Melon Seeds.

Sunday 17th.

I went to Church & heard prayers but no parson came to preach; I Bott. at Mr. Porters a Tin Tea Kettle one pint & one half pint stone mugg. Dined in Town & returned home in the afternoon notwithstanding a verry [hard?] rain.

Munday 18th.

Nil.

Tuesday 19th.

Do.

Wednesday 20th.

Do.

Thursday

This day the Stallions stable was finished.

Freiday 22d.

Nil.

Saturday 23d.

Planted 2 hills water melons.

Sunday 24th.

Dined at home & went to Snow creek Immediatly after. But John's going abroad oblidged me to return directly to school & upon coming up to the door I found it shut and Barrocaded on the inside. But after pushing, rapping with my foot & hollowing, I recd. no answer from within nor wou'd Anthy. Frazer oppen the door, Tho at the same time I cou'd see him & Lucy Gaines both covered up in bedd together.

My opinion of this courtship is in short this, That he never intends to marrie her, For as he does not at present propose staying here longer than this Year & the fall being the time proposed for there marriage he wants in the intrim to divert himself with her untill that time & then he'll make an excuse to her that he cannot Marrie while in Mr. Daingerfields employ, & so amuse himself with her untill his time is up: and once gone always gone, & so make a fool of her.

[*Page 135th*]   MUNDAY 25TH. MARCH 1776.

Genll. Muster in Town.

TUESDAY 26TH.

Mr. [&] Mrs. Daingerfield & Basset in Town last night, & the Anthy. Man of War Hugg & Hugg in great house bay all night. He & I at varriance about his behavour on Sunday.

WEDNESDAY 27TH.

Last night Mrs. Daingd. returned.

THURSDAY 28TH.

Last night the Lucy friggat Moored Hugg & Hugg alongside the Anthy. Man of [War?] in Blanket Bay within school cape. This day Anthony Frazer after having the Use of my Briddle for above six weeks took it off his Mare & verry ungenteely hung it in the Stallion's Stable, without either giving it me back or even so much as bringing it to school; But put it there with a design I supose that it might be wore out on the Stallion.

FREIDAY 29TH.

A. F. lost his Tongue, or tyed it.

SATURDAY 30TH.

Last night verry rainy, Yet Lucy at school Hugg & Hugg with Tony untill verry late and hade not a niger wench staid out for her wou'd have been all night in the same position. At 12 this day I went to Daniel Dempsie's & agreed with his wife to spin the 3 lb.

Cotton I carried there 27th. Jany. last to run 6 Yds. per lb. at 3/ per. This night Lucy at school again, and in the same situation with Tony as last night. He dumb to me still.

SUNDAY 31ST.

Rode to Church in compy. with Mr. Richards A. Frazer & Lucy. I heard sermon by Mr. Maryee his Text was in the 1st. Epl. Genll. of John 2d. Chp: & 15 V. I came home in the afternoon, A. F. when dark, & still dumb. Lucy stayed in Town all night with her Mother.

MUNDAY 1ST. APRIL.

Lucy in Town & A. F. dumb.

TUESDAY 2D.

Lucy still in Town & A. F. still dumb.

WEDNESDAY 3D.

Lucy still in Do. & A. F. still Do.

THURSDAY 4TH.

Lucy still in Do. & A. F. still Do.

FREIDAY 5TH.

This day I went to Church and heard Mr. Marye preach his Text in 53d C: Isah & 1st. part of the 3d. V. This afternoon Lucy came home, & was in school with the Anthony Man of War when I returned, & Moored there in Blanket Bay along side of him all night, he still dumb.

[*Page 136th*]   SATURDAY 6TH.

This morning as soon as the Anthony Man of War & the Lucy friggate unmoored he rigged himself & imediatly set of[f] for his Mothers, or God knows where, leaving the keys of the Barn with Lucy, and his people to look after themselves, he still dumb. The Colo. complaining verry loudly that his Plantation is greatly behind hand, which he thinks is owing to Anthonys courtship. At same time he told me if

he wou'd Marrie Lucy; he wou'd give him one upper room in the house, untill he was otherways provided.

Sunday 7th.

This morning Lucy ask'd me to walk to Mr. Becks with her & from that to Mr. Reyns's[132] which I did. But soon after we got to Mr. Reyns's, there came a boy with a Horse for me for to go & dine with Mr. McCauly[133] at his house six Miles distant, which I did and came home in the evening, after staying the afternoon there.

Munday 8th.

This morning rainie, & after Breackfast Lucy came to school & brought her own work with her & continued at it the whole day. She proposing to leave the place, as Mrs. Daingerfield & her are at present at varriance on Anthys. Accott. Lucy now begins to be something doubtfull of Anthys. Marr[y]ing her conform to his promise and seems resolved to put him to the push tomorrows night if he comes home, or at any rate before she leaves this.

TUESDAY 9TH.

This morning I keept school untill 11 AM when the Colo. Desired I wou'd ride to Town upon some bussiness. In my way there I met Anthony but no words betwixt us.

WEDNESDAY 10TH.

Last night Lucy wrote Anthy. a line to come down & speack to her, but after he went she hade not resolution enough to put him to the push, so matters stands betwixt them as they were.

THURSDAY 11TH.

Last night Lucy came to school with a pretence of bringing us some supper but did not stay above half an hour. No words betwixt him & me. This night Anthony dischd. himself from the Colos. employ by Missive.

[*Page 137th*]   FREIDAY 12TH. APRIL.

This morning Anthony, after putting his letter case & Jurnal in his pocket, went to Town where he staid all the day & night following. In the afternoon Lucy was sent for to see her Mother at three Miles distance. She is surprised Anthony did not see her before he went away, nor have a line for her. She begged me to give her compts. to him in case he shou'd return in her absence.

SATURDAY 13TH.

This morning Anthony returned here made friends with me, packed up his things & left them to my care untill sent for. But never so much as enquired for Lucy, so after he was got on horse back I followed him about a Hundd. yds. & delivd. her Message to him. His compts. to her again was all the return.

SUNDAY 14TH.

I went to Town in Compy. with Lucy, Mr. Richards & Mr. Heely. Imediatly after sermon, the above three set off together for Mr. Rich-ards. I went to Mr. Myles's[134] where I dined, and was desired by him to enquire at the Colo. if he wou'd Accept of him for an Overseer next year. Mrs. Gaines Lucy's Mother came here this afternoon.

Munday 15th.

Lucy verry disconsolate like.

Tuesday 16.

The Colo. & his Lady went over the River to King George this day, & staid there all night. At noon I set out for Town, dined with Mr. Fulton, got the Newspapers and then return'd. In my absence Mrs. Gaines had been sent for, Lucy still disconsolate, but I find she can now sleep in the great house with the Childreen by herself, that is without any other white person in the House. But all the time Mr. Frazer lived here, word always came to the school for one to go down & sleep in the House; & I have known him turned out of his bedd (short before his departure) to go down & sleep there or rather ly in bedd that she might court him while her eyes cou'd keep oppen & then go to sleep herself by him which I realy belive made him heartyly tyred of her at last: Nothwithstanding I truely think she is honest; but her over fondness of him, was her loseing of him.

[Page 138th]   Wednesday 17th. April 1776.

Miss Lucy is losing her stomach, she sat at the table with me this day but eat no dinner.

Thursday 18th.

Nothing remarcable this day.

Freiday 19th.

At 9 AM when I cam out from Breackfast I found Mr. Frazer in the school & soon after Miss Lucy came to it. At 11 I left the school & took the boys with me. They remained there by themselves untill 2 pm when he set off, & since Lucy seems to be in high spirits, so I hope the wind blows fair for [her?] yet.

Saturday 20th.

At noon I asked the Colo. for a bottle of rum as I expected two Countrymen to see me tomorrow, which he verry Cheerfully gave & desired me to ask him for one any time I wanted it & told me to take them to the Howse to dinner with me. In the afternoon he, his Lady,

& Daughter went over the river to Mr. Jones's[135] in King George county. Lucy continues cheerfull.

SUNDAY 21ST.

From 9 AM heavy rain all the day which stopt my Countrymen from coming. At 11 AM came here one John Richardson from the Gunnery[136] in Town and brought his mare to Ariell, had her covered twice paid me 20/ of the money & returd. in the evening; Lucy as Yesterdy.

MUNDAY 22D.

Mr. & Mrs. Daingerfield & their Daughter returned hom this day; Lucy living in good hopes.

TUESDAY 23D.

At noon rode to Town got the Newspapers, & settled with Mr. Porter for teaching his two sons 12 Mos. when he verry genteely allowed me £6 for them, besides a present of two silk Vests & two pair of Nankeen Breeche's last summer & a Gallon of rum at Christenmass, both he & Mrs. Porter being extreamly well satisfied with what I hade don to them. Lucy as Yesterdy.

WEDNESDAY 24TH.

General Muster of all the County Malitia in Town to day. At Breackfast the Colo. desired me to go & see it if I pleased, But being in Town yesterday I chose to stay to day with my boys. At noon Miss Lucy went to Mr. Richards, & returned to school a little after sun sett, in order to wait Mr. Frazer who [*Page 139*] hade appointed to meet her here this night; She staid chatting with me untill about ten OClock, but he being not come then she went down to the house, and on her ariviall she found the doors were shut & they all gone to bedd. So she was oblidged to return back to school, where she laid herself down in Mr. Frazers bedd with her cloaths on, was verry uneasy & fell a crying, thinking then, he used her extreamly ill in not keeping his word. I soathed & comforted her all I cou'd & as there was none in the school but her & me (I in the one Bedd & she in the other). I soon got her to talk pretty cheerfully; & we continued so untill one or two Clock as I supose when I fell asleep & continued so untill they came for corn to feed the horses in the morning when I got up & dressed, & soon after she got up being dress'd as yesterday. She then sat down to wait him this morning, being 25th. but at 8 AM when the boys came to school no word of him untill Edwin told us he was come here again to live & was then with the people, which we cou'd scarcely belive.

I am still more & more confirmed in my opinion that she is a tender hearted, agreeable, good girle & one that is strictly virtous, honest, & modest, without making any vain show of it; And that nothing but her excessive love for Anthy. Frazer after engaging with him; On the one hand and his putting off their Marriage longer then needfull on the other; has I say created her, all the trouble that opresses her, & Ill will of Mrs. Daingerfield into the bargain as she is likely to leave her place. She staid in school untill after Breackfast, in which time she wrote a letter to her Mother begging her to remove her a[s] soon as possible from this place.

THURSDAY 25TH.

What Edwin told this morning of Anthy. Frazers being with the people is truth, for after having cool'd he came & made up Matters with the Colo. & returd. to his service.

FREIDAY 26TH.

Miss Lucy has not as yet seen Mr. Frazer. This forenoon her Mother returned here.

[Page 140th] SATURDAY 27TH. APRIL 1776.

This afternoon I went to Christr. Becks & his wife promised to spin for me   lbs. Cotton to make me Vaistcoats. From this day I'm resolved not to mention any thing more here relaiting to Anthy. & Lucy for some time because it takes up too much room; but will note whatever is remarcable on a slip of paper by itself.

SUNDAY 28TH.

This day came here to pay me a Visit Mr. Reid from Mansfield & Mr. Scott from Toun & dined with me in the great house by the Colos. order, and after we hade spent the afternoon verry agreeably together they returned home in the evening.

Munday 29th.

I carried [?] lbs. Cotton to Mr. Becks.

Tuesday 30th.

Verry hard rain with wind thunder & Ligg.

Wednesday 1st. May.

Smart frost this night.

Thursday 2d.

I Planted 10 Hills water Melons.

Freiday 3d.

The Colo. began to plant Corn, still cold.

Saturday 4th.

At Mr. Becks in the afternoon.

Sunday 5th.

Early this morning I went to Mr. McCalley's & entred his oldest son (about 8 years of age) to writting. Stayed there all day & rode his horse home in the evening: The Colo. went to Newpost & dinned there.

Munday 6th.

Tuesday 7th.

Billie ended reading through his Bible.

Wednesdy. 8th.

At noon went with the boys to walk.

Thursday 9th.

After dinner I took the boys with me to Massaponacks Briges to see 56 prissoners that was taken at the late battle in North Carolina, among them was a great ma[n]y Emigrants from Scotland who were all officers. I talked with severals of them from Ross Shire and the Isle of Sky.[137]

FREIDAY 10TH.

Nothing remarcable.

SATURDAY 11TH.

After dinner went Mr. Becks.

[*Page 141st*]   SUNDAY 12TH. MAY 1776.

This forenoon I went to Dempsie's to see if my three pound of Cotton was spun but I found it was not begun too, nor will be in this month.

MUNDAY 13TH.

Nothing remarcable.

TUESDAY 14TH.

Do. . . . Do.

WEDNESDAY 15TH.

Mr. & Mrs. Daingerfield abroad.

THURSDAY 16TH.

Mr. & Mrs. Daingerfield Do.

FREIDAY 17TH.

Genll. Fast by order of the Congress.[138] I went to Church in Toun but no sermon. Dined at Mr. McAlleys & came home in the evening. The Colo. & his Lady at Mount Church.

SATURDAY 18TH.

I eat ripe Cherreys.

SUNDAY 19TH.

The Colo. his Lady & Anthony Frazer at Mount Church. After

breackfast I went over to King George & dined with Mrs. White & two of her daughters & returned home in the Afternoon. In the evening Miss Lucy came from Toun, having been there since Sunday last.

MUNDAY 20TH.

I eat green pease & ripe strawberries.

TUESDAY 21ST.

I bought ½ Gallon of Whiskie at 2/ 6.

WEDNESDAY 22D.

Company here.

THURSDAY 23D.

Mrs. Daingerfield abroad.

FREIDAY 24TH.

I bought 1 pair thd. stockins at 5/.

SATURDAY

I went to Toun to buy a hatt.

SUNDAY 26TH.

Being White sunday at home all day.

MUNDAY 27TH.

At 9 AM I went to Mr. McAlleys and staid teaching his son & sister untill dark & then rode home bringing with me 1½ Yd. Linen for summer breeches.

TUESDAY 28TH.

At Mr. Becks & Snow creek.

WEDNESDAY 29TH.

Bathurest 9 year old this day.

THURSDAY 30TH.

Made some snuff for Capt. Strother.[139]

FREIDAY 31ST.

I sent my Hatt to Toun by Jacob to be Dressed Cutt round & trimmed with binding.

[*Page 142d*]   SATURDAY 1ST. JUNE 1776.

I hade an Agu at night.

SUNDAY 2D.

At home all day. Compy. here.

MUNDAY 3D.

A fine rain all day.

TUESDAY 4TH.

Nothing remarcable.

WEDNESDAY 5TH.

No[th]ing Do.

THURSDAY 6TH.

In the afternoon I went to Mr. Becks, when he told me that Mrs. Battle[140] wanted to see me & to talk to me about teaching her two daughters to write, upon which I imediatly waited upon her & engaged to return upon Saturd. next by 1 pm & begin them to write but made no bargain as yet.

FREIDAY 7TH.

Nothing remarcable.

SATURDAY 8TH.

At noon I went to Mrs. Bataile's and entred two of her Daughters to writting, Viz. Miss Sallie and Miss Betty & continued teaching them until night, when I agreed to attend them every Saturday afternoon and every other Sunday from this date untill 8th. June 1777 (I[f] it please God to spare me) for four pound Virginia currancy.

SUNDAY 9TH.

After breackfast I rode to Mr. McAlleys & teach'd his son to write untill 4 pm & then came home in the evening.

MUNDAY 10TH.

Nothing remarcable.

TUESDAY 11TH.

Do. Do.

WEDNESDAY 12TH.

This forenoon came here one Nancy Holms & engaged to return & take her Station as a House-keeper, how soon Miss Lucy Gains is gone. At 6 pm I went to Mrs. Batailies & seed each of my Pupils write a page of (Quarto) paper.

THURSDAY 13TH.

Nothing remarcable.

FREIDAY 14TH.

At noon Went to Jno. McDearmans & had 6 Yds. stript Cotton warped for 2 Veastcoats and two handkerchiefs, all prepared at my own expence.

[Page 143d]   SATURDAY 15TH. JUNE 1776.

Yesterday morning the Colo. the Childreen & me began to eat bread & milk here for breackfast. At noon I went to Mrs. Battailes and teach'd writting until night conform to agreement.

SUNDAY 16TH.

At 10 AM I went to Dempsies to see if my Cotton was spun, but found they have not begun to do it, & as I find I can not depend on their word I must bring it away some time this week undone. I re-turn'd home to Dinner, and went to Snow creek in the afternoon.

MUNDAY 17TH.

Nothing remarcable.

TUESDAY 18TH.

Recd. a pair new shoes.

WEDNESDAY 19.

At noon went to Snow creek & the Boys & dined at the spring on Barbaque & fish. At 5 pm I went to Mrs. Battailes & teach'd untill ½ an hour past 7.

THURSDAY 20TH.

Nothing remarcable.

FREIDAY 21ST.

Nothing—Do.

SATURDAY 22D.

At noon carried 4 Yds. Cotton Jeans (I hade spun & wove here) to Mr. Becks to make me a short Coat for sumer wear, & then went to Mrs. Battailes and teach'd the rest of the afternoon, seed there at diner one Mrs. Morton[141] a Widow Lady from Albemarle, a pretty woman.

SUNDAY 23D.

I went before breackfast to Mr. McAlley's & teach'd his son till dinner after that spent most of the afternoon in Compy. with him, Mr. Reid at Mansfield & a Buckskin Reid, returned home in the evening.

MUNDAY 24TH.

Nothing Remarcable.

TUESDAY 25.

Nothing—Do.

WEDNESDAY 26.

At 5 pm I went to Mr. Becks & hade a short Coat cut out of cotton cloth wove Jeans. I bought the cotton and paid for spinning it at the rate of 2/6 per lb. and one shilling per Yd. for Weaving.

[*Page 144th*]   THURSDAY 27TH. JUNE 1776.

At 4 pm I went to Fredericksbg. & settled an Accott. of the Colos. with Jacob Whitely[142] & agreed to Whisque for the ballance at 6/ per gallon.

FREIDAY 28TH.

At 2 pm went to Town & received the Whisque from Jacob Whitely & 12 Gallons more from Mrs. Sullivan[143] at 5/ per Gallon.

Saturday 29th.

At noon I went to Mrs. Battailes & teached till near sundown, In which time there fel such a great quantity of rain Accompanyed with a verry hard gale of wind as rendred the runs impossible so I was obliged to go along with Harbine Moore[144] & stay at his House all night where I was verry genteely used.

Sunday 30th.

This day after breackfast I returned home where I stayed all day, it being verry hot, & the roads bad.

Munday 1st. July 1776.

Nothing remarcable.

Tuesday 2d.

Do. Do.

Wednesday 3d.

This afternoon I went to Mrs. Battailes & seed the young ladies write a page each. Same night recd. my short Coat made and paid 5/ for doing it.

Thursday 4th.

Nothing remarcable.

Freiday 5th.

Do. Do.

Saturday 6.

At noon went to Mrs. Battailes and teach'd untill sun down.

Sunday 7th.

This morning I rode to Mansfield and breackfast with Mr. Reid & stayed and dined with him and in the afternoon he and I rode to see the Rowgallies[145] that was building where we met with Mr. Anderson & Jacob Whitely and went to Town with them to Whitelys where we Joyned in Compy. with Mr. Wright & one Mr. Bruce[146] from King George. About 11 pm we brock up and every one went to his own home as I did.

MUNDAY 8TH.

This night came to School & stayed all night Anthy. Frazer's brother Jamie.[147]

[*Page 145th*]   TUESDAY 9TH. JULY 1776.

Nothing remarcable.

WEDNESDAY 10TH.

At 6 pm went to Mrs. Battaile's & teach'd until sunset and then returned home & soon after hea[r]d a great many Guns fired towards Toun. About 12 pm the Colo. Despatc[h]ed Anthy. Frazer there to see what was the cause of [it?] who returned, and informed him that there was great rejoicings in Toun on Accott. of the Congress having declared the 13 United Colonys of North America Independent of the Crown of great Britain.[148]

THURSDAY 11TH.

Nothing remarcable.

FREIDAY 12TH.

Do. Do.

SATURDAY 13TH.

At 11 AM I went to Mrs. Battaile's & teach'd untill about 7 pm and then returned home. This day I gave in my Accott. to Anthy. Frazer for payment.

SUNDAY 14.

This day came here Mr. & Mrs. Porter with all their Childreen & stayed all night.

MUNDAY 15TH.

Nothing remarcable this day.

TUESDAY 16TH.

Do. . . . . Do. this day.

WEDNESDAY 17TH.

Do. . . . . Do. I at Mrs. Battiles.

THURSDAY 18TH.

Do. . . . . Do. this day.

FREIDAY 19TH.

Do. . . . . Do. this day.

SATURDAY 20TH.

Do. . . . . Do. I at Mrs. Battiles.

SUNDAY 21ST.

I went to Mr. McAlleys & teach'd all day.

MUNDAY 22D.

This Morning Mrs. Gaines came here.

TUESDAY 23D.

This Morning Miss Lucy Do. left this place.

WEDNESDAY 24TH.

At ½ past 5 pm I went to Mrs. Battiles.

THURSDAY 25TH.

I imployed this morng. & forenoon getting Lead off Snow creek house.[149]

Freiday 26th.

Finished Wheat hearvest here this night.

Saturday 27th.

At noon I went to Mrs. Battailes.

Sunday 28th.

At 11 AM, I went to Mr. Thos. Miles's where I dined, & after dinner I went with Mr. & Mrs. Miles to the house of one Widdow McGumrey where we eat plumbs; & I bought thd. for a pair stockins from Nancy, an Irish girle at 2/ 6.

APPENDIXES

The original of the practice letter by Lucy Gaines (see opposite page). Courtesy Virginia Historical Society.

Appendix I

LUCY GAINES' LETTER*

Sr

my Mother desires that I should com up to morrow (if possible). [I] should be very glad if you will go to Mr becks this evening and ask Mrs. beck if she pleases to lend me her side Saddle to ride up to my Mother and you will Greatly oblige

March 9, 1776.   Your most humble Servt
                                         Lucy Gaines

The above is the first that ever Miss Lucy wrote by herself or without a Coppy, and I think it extreamly well put together for her first performance of the kind.

By practice she will Improve, Being naturally verry smart. J. H.

* Corbin Papers, Virginia Historical Society.

ANN HARROWER'S LETTER*

William Dangerfield Esqr.

Sir

Your two letters of the 14th. April 1777 Came to my hand in April 1778 and brought me the melancholy account of my dear Husbands death, an unhappy Event for me and my poor Children, but it is the will of God and we must submitt. My late dear husband in his different letters to me had given me such an oppinion of your kind dispositions to him, as gives me no reason to doubt but that all possible Care has been taken of him in his last illness in your Hospitable Family, but diseases of that kind baffles all the power of medicine. Had he been spaired to have been settled any time in the place you had appointed for him, he might no doubt been in a way of doing something for his family, and I well know that he would not have been ungrateful to his Benifactor, but death puts an End to all our prospects on this side the grave. You are pleased to tell me in your letter that you want to remitt me Seventy pound Sterling, which I Consider as an act of your generosity as I know my late husband had not any thing but what came from you. The unhappy difference that still subsists betwixt Great Brittan and America makes it difficult to advise how money from America is to be remitted to Brittan. Soon after the receipt of your two letters I wrote you—under cover to Messrs. Anderson & Horseburgh Merchants in Glasgow—but have not heard from them since, and Conclude my letter has not Come to your hand; Could the money any how been remitted to them it would Come safe to my hands; but as I am told that it may be more Convenient for you to have it remitted by way of holland, or Hamburgh, I have sent you two letters under cover to Messrs. Craufurd & Co. Merchants in Rotterdam and advised them to send the letter by two different ships bound for America, in hopes one of the letters may come to your hands. If you find it convenient to remitt the money to that house please ad-

* Mrs. Ann Harrower, Lerwick, May 24, 1780, to Colonel William Daingerfield, Accession No. 24981, Archives Division, Virginia State Library.

vise them to put it to the Acctt. of my Brother James Craigie
merchant in Lerwick Zetland, or if to Hamburgh to Mr. Richard
Thornton, if to Either of those hoses it will Come [safe] to my
hand. I am with the highest regard for you and [fa]mily Dear Sir
[Yo]ur most aff. & ob[edient] Servt.

Lerwick 24*th* May, 1780
[A]nn Harrower

[P.S.]

If this letter Comes to the hands of any British Officer it is hum-
bly hoped that in Compation to a poor Widdow He will forward
it as directed.

Appendix II

AN ACCOUNT of all Persons who have taken their passage on Board any Ship or Vessel, to go out of this Kingdom from any Port in England with a description of their Age, Quality, Occupation or Employment. former residence, to what port or place they propose to go, & on what Account, & for what purposes they leave the Country. from the 7th to the 13th February 1774. distinguishing each Port.*

EMBARKED from the PORT OF LONDON.

NAMES	AGE	QUALITY, OCCUPATION, OR EMPLOYMENT.	FORMER RESIDENCE
Francis Simpson	22	Glass Blower	Surry
John Broomfield	36	Stocking Weaver	Hereford
George Wild	21	Groom	York
Benjamin Badger	22	Husbandman	Do.
William Payne	21	Clerk & Bookkeeper	London
James Sutherland	18	Cordwainer	Do
Edwd. Fitzpatrick	31	Surgeon	Do
George Adams	25	Husbandman	Derby
Willm. Coventry	27	Ropemaker	Southwark
John Connery	40	Perukemaker	Do.
Alexr. Burnett	25	Clerk & Bookkeeper	Westminster

NAMES	AGE	QUALITY, OCCUPATION, OR EMPLOYMENT.	FORMER RESIDENCE
John Tran	20	Carpenter & Joiner	Southwark
James Packer	20	Founder	London
Edwd. Dougharty	20	Gardner	Do
George Boorer	24	Clerk & Bookkeeper	Do
Frederick Pampe	22	Watch & Clockmaker	Do
Mark Mitchell	19	Perukemaker	Do
James Owen	21	Bricklayer	Do
Robert Cowdell	17	Stocking Weaver	Leicester
Law Bagnall	28	Bucklemaker	Birmingham
John Turner	27	Cordwainer	London
John Kennelly	21	Bricklayer	Do
William Dunn	36	Do	Durham
Roger Nichols	40	Breeches Maker	Wilts
Joseph Ormond	24	Hatt Maker	Middlesex
Thomas Rand	22	Butcher	Ireland
William Sibery	47	Weaver	London
Peter Cooley	38	Do	Do
Peter Cooley junr.	18	Do	Do
John Cooley	16	Do	Do
Joseph Cooley	12	Do	Do
Robert Innis	23	Groom	Bristol
Benjamin Ogle	23	Pipemaker	Newcastle
James Freeman	20	Blacksmith	Northampton
Benjamin Thompson	27	Clock & Watchmaker	London
Richard Harris	29	Husbandman	Worcester
Daniel Lakenan	22	Cabinet maker	London
William Wood	29	Husbandman	Northampton
John Harrower	40	Clerk & Bookkeeper	Shetland
Thomas Ford	32	Carver & Gilder	London
John Williams	27	Husbandman	Do
Joseph Clark	21	Cordwainer	Do
Charles Avery	38	White Smith	Do
Thomas Richards	22	Perukemaker	Do
Edward Lawrance	41	Gardner	Middlesex
Thomas Low	17	Cabinet Maker	Chester
Mathew Fright	33	Husbandman	Kent
Peter Collins	40	Cordwainer	London

NAMES	AGE	QUALITY, OCCUPATION, OR EMPLOYMENT.	FORMER RESIDENCE
Alexander Kenneday	38	Cooper	Southwark
John Burton	22	Bricklayer	Ireland
Henry Newland	22	Silk Weaver	London
Thomas Rackstrow	38	Taylor	Do
James Nowland	38	Bricklayer	Do
Alexander Steward	21	Footman	Do
Charles Leslie	37	Taylor	Do
William Bradley	34	Tilemaker & Burner	London
Peter Woillidge	24	Painter & Glazier	Suffolk
William Phillips	41	Baker	London
John Sanders	15	Husbandman	Essex
Jeremiah Stacey	19	Linen Weaver	London
Richard Green	35	Farmer	Lincoln
Daniel Turner	22	Groom	London
John Bateman	23	Clerk & Bookkeeper	Westmoreland
John Goldin	25	Weaver	Wilts
Roger Wren	17	Cooper	London
James Downes	29	Husbandman	Do
John Mitchel	23	Smith & Farrier	Bristol
Thomas Davis	40	Husbandman	London
Henry Featson	22	Bricklayer	Southwark
John Powell	36	Boat Builder	Do
William Hudson	20	Linen Weaver	London
Samuel Mitchel	24	Cooper	York
Thomas Progers	23	Cordwainer	London
William Salton	42	Gardener	Middlesex
Harman Hester	44	Do.	London
			75 to Virginia

to what port or place Bound-Virginia
by what Ship–Planter
Masters Name–Daniel Bowers.
for what purpose they leave the Country–Indented Servants for
  Four Years.

* Treasury–Registers, Various–Weekly Emigration Returns, 1773–1774, P. R. O., T. 47/9, 54–57. Unpublished Crown-copyright material in the Public Record Office, London, has been reproduced by permission of the Controller of H. M. Stationery Office.

NOTES

Notes

INTRODUCTION

1. For studies of indentured servitude, see James Curtis Ballagh, *White Servitude in the Colony of Virginia: A Study of the System of Indentured Labor in the American Colonies* (Baltimore, 1895); Philip Alexander Bruce, *Economic History of Virginia in the Seventeenth Century* (2 vols., New York, 1907); Marcus Wilson Jernegan, *Laboring and Dependent Classes in Colonial America, 1607–1783* (Chicago, 1931); and Abbot Emerson Smith, *Colonists in Bondage: White Servitude and Convict Labor in America, 1607–1776* (Chapel Hill, 1947).

2. Harrower's situation was probably like that of William Bain, a shopkeeper in Caithness, who sailed for North Carolina in April, 1774, "because he could not get bread in his employment, the Poverty of the Common People" with whom he dealt "disabling them to pay their debts." Viola Root Cameron (comp.), *Emigrants from Scotland to America, 1774–1775, Copied from a Loose Bundle of Treasury Papers in the Public Record Office, London, England* (Baltimore, 1959), p. 16.

3. For information on Scottish emigration to the American Colonies, see Ian Charles Cargill Graham, *Colonists from Scotland: Emigration to North America, 1707–1783* (Ithaca, N.Y., 1956); A. R. Newsome (ed.), "Records of Emigrants from England and Scotland to North Carolina, 1774–1775," *North Carolina Historical Review*, XI (1934), 39–54, 129–143; and Margaret I. Adam, "The Highland Emigration of 1770," *Scottish Historical Review*, XVI (1918–1919), 280–293.

4. Graham, *Colonists from Scotland*, pp. 67–68.

5. For information about early Fredericksburg and Falmouth, see Oscar H. Darter, *Colonial Fredericksburg and Neighborhood in Perspective* (New York, 1957); Alvin T. Embrey, *History of Fredericksburg, Virginia* (Richmond, 1937); "Fredericksburg in Revolutionary Days," *William and Mary Quarterly*, 1st ser., XXVII (1918), 71–95, 164–175, 248–257.

6. For advertisements of the theatre in Fredericksburg, see the *Virginia Gazette*, April 30, 1752, and (Purdie & Dixon), May 16, 1771; of balls, see *ibid.*

(Rind), Dec. 11, 1766, Dec. 24, 1767, and (Dixon), Feb. 26, 1780; and of concerts, see *ibid*. (Rind), Dec. 24, 1767.

7. Daingerfield's grandfather, Colonel William Daingerfield of Greenfield, married Elizabeth, the daughter of Lancelot Bathurst of New Kent County who was the son of Sir Edward Bathurst. He was for many years a leading citizen of Essex County, serving as a justice of the peace, coroner, and county lieutenant of the militia, and representing Essex in the House of Burgesses. William's father, Edwin, married Hannah Bassett, the daughter of Colonel William Bassett of Eltham, and moved to New Kent County. He never acquired the position in society or politics held by his father, but he did serve as a vestryman and churchwarden for Blisland Parish and was a captain and later major in the county militia. *William and Mary Quarterly*, 1st ser., VIII (1899), 96–98; IX (1901), 188–189. Two Colonel William Daingerfields, first cousins, lived in Spotsylvania County at the same time. The other gentleman was Colonel William Daingerfield of Coventry (died 1781) who married Mary Willis. He was a vestryman of St. George's Parish, a justice of the county court, and an officer in the French and Indian War and the American Revolution.

8. William Daingerfield was chosen a vestryman of Blisland Parish, November 12, 1762, and served actively until he moved to Spotsylvania. C. G. Chamberlayne (ed.), *The Vestry Book of Blisland (Blissland) Parish, New Kent and James City Counties, Virginia, 1721–1786* (Richmond, 1935), pp. 157, 166, 167, 170, 172, 175, 185. He was listed as a justice of the New Kent County Court in the mid-1760's. Edward Ingle (comp.), "Justices of the Peace of Colonial Virginia," *Bulletin of the Virginia State Library*, XIV (1921), 60, 72, 78. He must also have been named commander of the county militia in 1764 or 1765 for his title, as

recorded in the vestry book of the parish, changed from "Mr." to "Col." There are no extant records to confirm his military service.

9. These letters from Athawes to Daingerfield between 1765 and 1768 are published in Wm. P. Palmer, *et al.* (eds.), *Calendar of State Papers and Other Manuscripts Preserved in the Capitol at Richmond, 1652–1781* (11 vols., Richmond, 1875–1893), I, 258–260.

10. The vestry, on October 23, 1770, chose "Mr. John Townes . . . in the stead of Col. William Daingerfield, who is removed out of the Parish." Chamberlayne, *Vestry Book of Blisland Parish*, p. 185.

11. William Armstrong Crozier (ed.), *Virginia County Records, Spotsylvania County, 1721–1800* . . . (New York, 1905), p. 365. (Hereafter cited as Crozier, *Spotsylvania County*). Sarah Taliaferro was the sole heir of her father. *William and Mary Quarterly*, 1st ser., XVII (1908), 65–66.

12. Belvidera was a rectangular, brick, two-story house of the simple design characteristic of rural dwellings in the Tidewater. An unusual feature was the ornamentation of the windows with rusticated stone segmental heads and stone sills. The interior followed the general layout of similar Virginia homes of that period. On the first floor the central passageway opened into a parlor and a dining room on the one side, and on the other into "the Chamber," which served as the master bedroom, linen storage room, office, and family room. A walnut stairway led from the passage to three bedrooms and a nursery on the upper floor. With the exception of the room occupied during Harrower's time by Lucy Gaines, the housekeeper, the bedrooms were used by the children of the family. (The interior arrangement of the house is taken from the inventory and appraisal of Colonel Daingerfield's estate which listed the personal property by rooms. Spotsylvania County Will Book E, 1772–1798, 590–592). When

Alexander Berger, father of the present proprietor Mrs. Helen (Berger) Bryan, acquired the estate in 1909, he added dormers, thus making it a two-and-a-half story house. Sue K. Gordon, Report on Belvidera (1937), Works Progress Administration, Virginia Historical Inventory, Virginia State Library; recollections of Mrs. C. S. Hooper of Fredericksburg and Mrs. George Watson of Alexandria.

13. Daingerfield eschewed most public offices in Spotsylvania. He did serve as an overseer of the road near his plantation and was paid for building a bridge over Massaponax Creek on June 18, 1772. Spotsylvania County Order Book [Minutes], 1768–1774. "William Daingerfield (on Rapahanock)" was recommended as a justice of the peace by the county court on June 20, 1772, but he refused to qualify. *Ibid.;* his refusal was noted at a meeting of the Council of Virginia on May 7, 1773 in Journal of the Council, P. R. O., C. O. 5/1432, 29. He was appointed to the vestry on November 24, 1780, but did not qualify for this office before the county court until May 16, 1782. St. George's Parish Vestry Book, II, 126 (Ms. in Alderman Library of the University of Virginia); Spotsylvania County Order Book [Minutes], 1774–1782.

14. See Lewis Cecil Gray, *History of Agriculture in the Southern United States to 1860* (2 vols., New York, 1941), I, 161–176. (Hereafter cited as Gray, *Agriculture*).

15. Nathaniel Burwell to his brother, June 13, 1718, in *William and Mary Quarterly*, 1st ser., VII (1898), 43–44. See also Louis B. Wright, *The First Gentlemen of Virginia* (San Marino, 1940), pp. 95–116, and Philip Alexander Bruce, *Institutional History of Virginia in the Seventeenth Century* (2 vols., New York, 1910), I, 293–330.

16. Jonathan Boucher, *View of Causes and Consequences of the American Revolution* (London, 1797), pp. 183–184.

17. Hunter Dickinson Farish (ed.), *Journal & Letters of Philip Vickers Fithian, 1773–1774: A Plantation Tutor of the Old Dominion* (Williamsburg, 1957), pp. 29, 94.

18. William Beverley to Micajah Perry, July 8, 1741, in *William and Mary Quarterly*, 1st ser., XIX (1911), 145.

19. The instruction of a deaf mute must have tried all of Harrower's ingenuity. What methods he devised, we can only guess. John Bolling of Cobbs, Virginia, also a deaf mute, was sent to Thomas Braidwood's school in Edinburgh in 1771 and did not return until 1781. It is highly improbable that Harrower knew Braidwood's carefully kept secrets of instruction. Whatever methods he used, they were most successful. After six months of instruction, John Edge was able to write "mostly for any thing he wants," to understand figures, and to work "single addition a little." Apparently Harrower did not attempt to teach him to speak. Edward Miner Gallaudet, "History of the Education of the Deaf in the United States," *American Annals of the Deaf*, XXXI (1886), 130–147; Francis Earle Lutz, *Chesterfield, an old Virginia County* (Richmond, 1954), pp. 158–159.

20. Harrower's journal is an excellent source for a student of dialects. His phonetic spelling can provide clues to the pronunciation of words, especially the names of places and persons, in the eighteenth century. There are many indications of the broadness of his speech in his writings; e.g., the consistent use of the double "r" in "very," "mace" for "mess," "mate" for "meat," etc.

21. Colonel Daingerfield dispatched the melancholy news to Ann Harrower in two letters on April 14, 1777, but they were not received by her until a year later. These letters and several replies by the widow have been lost. Finally, a letter written by Mrs. Harrower over three years after her husband's death reached Virginia. Although not delivered, it did survive.

See Ann Harrower's letter to Colonel Daingerfield, May 24, 1780, appearing in Appendix I. The letter was called to the attention of the editor by William J. Van Schreeven, State Archivist of Virginia.

22. Advertisement in *Virginia Gazette* (Dixon & Hunter), Dec. 5, 1777.

23. Arthur Lee to Colonel Theodorick Bland, September 27, 1781, in Charles Campbell (ed.) *The Bland Papers* (2 vols., Petersburg, 1840–1843), II, 77. The hay was undoubtedly purchased by the French cavalry on their way to Yorktown. A map by an unknown French cartographer depicting the line of march and the camp sites of Rochambeau's army from Newport to Yorktown locates the residence of "Colonel dangerfield." Francois Soulés, *Histoire des Troubles de l'Amérique Anglaise* (4 vols., Paris, 1787), IV, Map 1.

24. In February, 1782, Daingerfield was forced to borrow £1,000 from James Mercer of Fredericksburg and secure the debt with 1,300 acres of his wife's lands on Snow Creek. Crozier, *Spotsylvania County*, 365. He was able to repay the debt within a month, yet, on August 2, 1782, he sold his New Kent property to William Claiborne. This transaction only intensified his financial problems. In the following January he told a friend "that he was in Dainger of loosing the Tobacco for which he had sold his Land in New Kent." Unfortunately the early deed books of New Kent County have not survived, and the details of the sale cannot be ascertained. The date of the sale is recorded in the memorandum of conveyances at the end of the land tax list of 1782 in New Kent County Tax Lists, 1782–1810, Archives Division, Virginia State Library. Alexander Denholm's deposition, dated August 31, 1785, describes a conversation with Colonel Daingerfield on January 3, 1783. Spotsylvania County Manuscript Loose Wills, A–D (microfilm copy in Archives Division, Virginia State Library). Denholm had lived for

several years at Belvidera; he may have been the tutor there after Harrower. A Mr. Denholm was listed as a teacher in Fredericksburg before 1781 in the records of Trinity College, Cambridge. *Virginia Magazine of History and Biography*, XXI (1913), 82.

25. Will recorded in Spotsylvania County Will Book E, 1772–1798, 37. Daingerfield left his estate to his wife until her remarriage or death, when it was to be equally divided among his children. Mrs. Daingerfield was named "sole Executor" but was advised to employ William Smith of King William County to assist her. In a note added to the will Daingerfield asked his half-brother William Allen also to act as executor. Their mother, Hannah Bassett, first married Joseph Allen, and later Edwin Daingerfield. See copy of will of Martha Corran, dated September 24, 1804, in papers of U. S. Circuit Court, Virginia District, Ended Cases, Patrick Corran vs. Corran's Executors & Heirs, 1821, in Archives Division, Virginia State Library. Martha Corran was Colonel Daingerfield's sister; her first husband was Dr. Theodorick Bland. In a deposition concerning the will, William Allen stated that he was "only a collateral heir of Martha Corran." Daingerfield's will was renounced by his widow, who was awarded "the Belvidera Tract of Land" by the county court as her dower right. When William Allen refused to serve, General Spotswood volunteered as executor of the estate. Spotsylvania County Order Book, 1782–1786, 34, 39.

26. John Melville Jennings (ed.), "Letters of James Mercer to John Francis Mercer," *Virginia Magazine of History and Biography*, LIX (1951), 92.

Newcastle was a small town on the Pamunkey River in Hanover County. In 1748 it was considered by the House of Burgesses as a desirable site for the Capital of Virginia after the destruction by fire of the Capitol in Williamsburg. The town is now extinct. Malcolm H. Harris, "The Port Towns of the Pamunkey," *William and Mary Quarterly*, 2nd ser., XXIII (1943), 503–510.

The appraisement of the personal property of the estate listed 68 slaves valued at £3,085, and livestock worth £468/15. The total value of the personal property was appraised at £3,854/19/2. This was not an inconsiderable estate. The loss of the tobacco for which he sold his New Kent land was not sufficient to bankrupt him. Apparently he had become mentally unbalanced by worry from unknown causes.

Sarah (Taliaferro) Daingerfield died sometime prior to 1796. Upon her death the estate was divided among the heirs by a decree of the High Court of Chancery. See deed of Samuel Moseley and his wife Hannah Bassett to Francis T. Brooke, August 30, 1796, in Crozier, *Spotsylvania County*, 488–489. The records of the High Court of Chancery have been destroyed, but a deed, accompanied by a plat showing the division of the Belvidera tract among the heirs, was recorded in the Fredericksburg District Court in 1805. Fredericksburg District Court Deed Book E, 1803–1806, 344–346. Edwin, the eldest son, received the mansion house and a sizeable tract. Deed Book KK, 1842–1844, 105–107. Thus Belvidera was lost to the Daingerfield family.

JOURNAL

1. Harrower lived at Twageos, a small community practically contiguous to Lerwick at that time. Lerwick, the capital of Shetland, was described in 1774 as "a small irregularly built village, containing about 140 families. . . ." Tour of the Rev. George Low reprinted in James M. Crawford, *The Parish of Lerwick: An Ecclesiastical and Historical Sketch* (Lerwick, 1901), p. 14. A visitor some years later stated that the town "consists of one principal street next the quay, with several lanes branching off. No regularity has been observed, in former times, in the position of the houses, some of which project almost quite across the street." Patrick Neill, *A Tour Through Some of the Islands of Orkney and Shetland* . . . (Edinburgh, 1806), p. 68.

2. Shetland stockings were famous and an important article of export. Traffic with the Dutch fishing fleet in woolen goods was especially heavy. The Rev. George Low wrote in 1774: "The whole time the fleet lay, the country people flocked to Lerwick with loads of coarse stockings, gloves, night-caps, rugs, and a very few articles of fresh provisions. Several thousands of pounds are annually drawn from the first article, though a pair of stockings seldom sells for more than 6d or 8d." Low, quoted in Crawford, *Parish of Lerwick*, p. 33. In the Rev. James Sands's account of the parish in 1791, he stated: "The only manufacture carried on in the parish is the knitting of woollen stockings, and in this almost all the women are more or less engaged." *Ibid.*, p. 37.

3. Anker, a dry measure, as an anker of potatoes, one-third of a barrel. Thomas Edmondston, *An Etymological Glossary of the Shetland Orkney Dialect* (London, 1866), p. 3.

4. The sons of the Rev. John Barclay, minister of Delting. The two boys were apparently going to the University of Aberdeen. Patrick received his M.A. degree from King's College, Aberdeen, in 1775, and then served as the minister at Sandsting from 1781 until his resignation in 1812. Robert became Lt. Col. Sir Robert Barclay, K.C.B. Hew Scott, *Fasti Ecclesiae Scoticanae: The Succession of Ministers in the Church of Scotland from the Reformation* (7 vols., Edinburgh, 1915–1928), VII, 307 and 315.

5. William Maule, Viscount Maule of Whitechurch and Earl of Panmure

of Forth, was colonel of the 62nd Dragoons (Royal Scots Grays) from 1770 until his death in 1782. *Dictionary of National Biography* (63 vols., London, 1894), XXXVII, 87 (hereafter cited as *DNB*); *The Gentleman's Magazine, and Historical Chronicle . . . For the Year MDCCLXXXI*, LI, 442. John Maule, his younger brother, was a member of Parliament and one of the Barons of the Court of Exchequer in Scotland from 1760 until his death in 1781. *DNB*, XXXVII, 86.

6. John Harrower, merchant of Lerwick, was admitted to the Morton Lodge of Freemasons in Lerwick on January 14, 1765. He later served as Junior Warden and a member of the committee to direct the finishing of the new building for the Lodge. (The records of the Morton Lodge were searched by Mr. John J. Graham, Lerwick.)

7. Harrower frequently confused the letters "v" and "w." He obviously meant NW (northwest) here. Later in the journal the reader must read "river Wear" for "river Vear," "vomit" for "womite," etc. The bearing V.B.S. should be read as west by south.

8. Probably a relative of Samuel Scollay, a merchant of Lerwick. See "Annals of Lerwick, Kirk Session Records of May 23, 1770," *Shetland Times*, May 7, 1898.

9. Happisburgh (pronounced Haisburgh) Church, a well-known landmark, stands high on the coast midway between Cromer and Yarmouth. Shipping at this point is usually not far from the coast. (The church was identified by Mr. Thomas F. Barton, Norwich, England.)

10. A Scottish word for a thin layer of turf or peat.

11. The road from Portsmouth to London may be followed by referring to "A Map of the ROADS from LONDON to PORTSMOUTH, CHICHESTER . . ." in *The Gentleman's Magazine for June 1765*, XXXV, 301. Harrower's phonetic spelling can be easily deciphered; from Portsmouth he walked through Portsdown, Horndean, Petersfield, Rake, Liphook, Godalming, Guilford, Merrow, Horsley, Effingham, Leatherhead, Ashtead, Epsom, and Wandsworth to London.

12. In Wapping, near the London docks.

13. The Rag Fair, an old clothes market held in Rosemary Lane (now Royal Mint Street), Whitechapel, was the subject of a drawing by Thomas Rowlandson. See Bernard Falk, *Thomas Rowlandson: His Life and Art* (New York, 1952), p. 60; William Addison, *English Fairs and Markets* (London, 1953), pp. 75-76.

14. Cunningsburgh, a village about eight miles south of Lerwick. The name Halcrow appears frequently in the documents printed as appendixes to Gilbert Goudie (ed.), *Diary of the Reverend John Mill, Minister of the Parishes of Dunrossness, Sandwick and Cunningsburgh in Shetland, 1740-1803* . . . (Edinburgh, 1889).

15. The Jamaica Coffee-House in St. Michael's Alley, Cornhill, was near the Royal Exchange and a noted subscription house for merchants and captains engaged in the West Indies trade. *Virginia Magazine of History and Biography*, XXVII (1919), 372.

16. Somerset House was not the building now so called, but its predecessor, the old mansion of the Protector, Edward Seymour, Duke of Somerset. The building devolved to the crown upon the attainder of Somerset in 1662. In the 1770's it was "occasionally used for the Reception and Entertainment of Foreign Princes and Ambassadors; as its pleasant Walks and beautiful Bowling-Green are for the Diversion of the Citizens." William Maitland, *The History of London . . .* (2 vols., London, 1775), II, 1346. See John Summerson, *Georgian London* (New York, 1946), p. 46 *et seq.*, for descriptions of buildings as seen by Harrower.

17. Purl is a liquor made by infusing wormwood or other bitter herbs in

ale or beer. *Oxford English Dictionary* . . . (12 vols., Oxford, 1933). (Hereafter cited as *OED*).

18. Robert Irvine of Lerwick petitioned the Kirk Session on October 5, 1770, "for a small matter out of the poors' funds to be given for burying the Corps of Mrs. Robertson in this parish (Relict of Mr. Walter Robertson, Late School Mr.)." The Kirk Session gave twelve shillings to Irvine for this purpose. "Annals of Lerwick," *Shetland Times*, May 14, 1898. Mr. Robertson, clerk of the Kirk Session and schoolmaster, had been in in straitened circumstances in 1762 because of the small number of scholars in his school. The Kirk Session in that year allowed him an additional eight shillings sterling out of the poors' money. *Ibid.*, Dec. 4, 1897.

19. The harbor of Lerwick. The Rev. George Low described the harbor in the summer of 1774: "The village commonly called the town of Lerwick is situate on a sound of the sea, formed by the island of Brassa, and thence the name; capable of containing many hundreds of ships, at this time there were about 400 Busses of several nations, as Danes, Prussians, French, Ostenders, but the greatest number Dutch, whose share amounted to upwards of 200 sail; with *two* English and one *Scotch* Vessel, and one belonging to the town, all these on the herring fishery." *Ibid.*, June 25, 1898. A buss was a two- or three-masted vessel (of various sizes) used especially in the Dutch herring-fishing. *OED*.

20. The entries of February 7, May 17, 23, and 25, 1774, prove that the entries down to May 25, 1774, are not contemporary, but a passage in a letter of August 7, 1774, seems to indicate that daily notes were made by Harrower.

21. A snow resembled a brig, carrying a main and foremast and a supplementary trysail mast close behind the mainmast. Snows were usually larger vessels than brigs or brigantines. *OED*.

22. John Bruce Stewart of Symbister and Bigton, an important proprietor in the south of Shetland. Goudie, *Diary of the Reverend John Mill*, pp. 22, 151, *et seq.* Alexander Steward, 21 years of age, was a footman from London according to the list of servants sailing on the *Planter*. Treasury–Registers, Various–Weekly Emigration Returns, 1773–1774, Public Record Office, Treasury 47/9, 54–57. (See Appendix for a copy of this list of indentured servants on board the *Planter*).

23. Alexander Burnett, 25, was a clerk and bookkeeper from Westminster; Samuel Mitchell, a cooper, was 24 years of age.

24. Mess. It was customary to provide for feeding servants during the voyage by dividing them into "messes" of four, five, six or more persons, and allotting food in fixed amounts to each mess. Smith, *Colonists in Bondage*, p. 212.

25. Alexander Kennedy, 38, was the only servant with whom Harrower appears to have developed a lasting friendship. Kennedy settled in Fredericksburg and frequently visited Harrower. Apparently he continued his craft as a cooper after serving out his indenture, for he presented a certificate dated April 20, 1782 to the Spotsylvania County Court for £55 Specie "for Cooperage." Spotsylvania County Order Book [Minutes], 1782–1786, 48.

26. Possibly Mark Mitchell, 19 years of age.

27. Note the large number of skilled craftsmen among the indentured servants on board the *Planter*. (See Appendix.)

28. Harrower's spelling of place names was phonetic. "Greenage" for "Greenwich" can be understood, but more difficult is "Ullage" for "Woolwich."

29. Indented.

30. A possible interpretation of this abbreviation would be "close-reefed topsails."

31. Geneva (Dutch: *jenever*) was Holland gin.

32. Ague.

33. A possible interpretation is "blue boil." Blue is a colloquialism meaning indecent or obscene. *OED*.

34. Sharks.

35. Piltock is the name in Shetland of the coalfish in its second year. *OED*.

36. The *York* arrived in the York River on May 12, 1774. *Virginia Gazette* (Purdie & Dixon), May 12, 1774.

37. John Powell, 36 years of age, from Southwark, England.

38. Urbanna, in Middlesex County, was named in honor of Queen Anne. It was an important port of entry.

39. Hobb's Hole (now Tappahannock), in Rappahannock (now Essex) County, was designated one of the port towns of Virginia by the General Assembly in 1680. William Waller Hening (ed.), *The Statutes at Large; Being a Collection of All the Laws of Virginia* . . . (13 vols., Richmond, 1809–1823), II, 473. (Hereafter cited as Hening, *Statutes*); Edward M. Riley, "The Town Acts of Colonial Virginia," *Journal of Southern History*, XVI (1950), 311–312. Fifty acres were surveyed for a town to be named New Plymouth, but apparently this name was never used. The town received the more euphonious name of Tappahannock in the short-lived "Act for establishing ports and towns" passed by the General Assembly in 1706 and repealed by royal proclamation in 1710. Hening, *Statutes*, V, 304–305. The early name, Hobb's Hole, persisted throughout the eighteenth century despite its lack of glamour.

40. The town of Leeds was established in King George (now Westmoreland) County by an act of Assembly in 1742 as a result of "great numbers of people" settling at Bray's Church near the public warehouses. Hening, *Statutes*, V, 193–197. It was an important mercantile center until after the Revolution. It was also famous for its horse races. *Virginia Gazette*, Aug. 14, 1746; (Purdie & Dixon), Sept. 9, 1773. Leedstown is chiefly noted as the site of the historic meeting, February 27, 1766, of the leading planters in the Northern Neck when resolutions condemning the Stamp Act where adopted. *Ibid.* (Rind), May 16, 1766; see also David W. Eaton, *Historical Atlas of Westmoreland County, Virginia* (Richmond, 1942), p. 14 *et seq.*

41. Port Royal on the Rappahannock River in Caroline County was established by an act of the Assembly in 1744. Hening, *Statutes*, V, 287–292. The excellent harbor at Port Royal could accommodate vessels drawing up to eleven feet of water. It prospered as one of the principal markets in the colony for tobacco, wheat, and corn but declined after the American Revolution. Joseph Martin (comp.), *A New and Comprehensive Gazetteer of Virginia* . . . (Charlottesville, 1835), p. 143.

42. Morton's Landing was located on the Rappahannock River in King George County. See plat of property in King George Deed Book No. 19, 304; also George H. S. King (comp.), *The Register of Overwharton Parish, Stafford County, Virginia; 1723–1758* (published by the compiler, 1961), p. 216.

43. Fredericksburg was established in 1727 by an act of the General Assembly. Fifty acres purchased from John Royston and Robert Buckner were surveyed into town lots. Hening, *Statutes*, IV, 234–239. Colonel William Byrd visited the town in 1732 and noted: "Tho' this be a commodious and beautiful Situation for a Town, with the Advantages of a Navigable River, and wholesome Air, yet the Inhabitants are very few." Byrd, "A Progress to the Mines" in John Spencer Bassett (ed.), *The Writings of Colonel William Byrd of Westover in Virginia Esq.* (New York, 1901), p. 373. With the development of the Piedmont in the mid-1700's, Fredericksburg flourished as a trade center and transshipment point for the interior. The county court was moved to Fredericksburg in 1732, and the town's rapid growth was shown in the en-

larging of its boundaries in 1759 and again in 1769. Hening, *Statutes*, IV, 364; VII, 314–315; VIII, 418–419.

44. Daniel Turner, 22, was a groom from London.

45. Easdale or Eisdale, a small island among the Hebrides, entirely composed of slate and at this time famous for its quarries.

46. Harrower's description is confirmed by the prison bounds established by the county court on December 17, 1773. The bounds included two squares as follows: ". . . the Square on which the Church & Market House stand, the Square on which the Court House, Prison, Mr. Geo. Mitchells, Jno. Atkinsons, Thos. James's and where Hugh Houstons Houses stand. . . ." Spotsylvania County Order Book [Minutes], 1768–1774. The Market or Town House was a center of social activity in colonial Fredericksburg. When he visited the town in May, 1777, Ebenezer Hazard noted: "Even this small Town affords a Proof of the Luxury & Extravagance of its Inhabitants, for a House has been erected by private Subscription, which is entirely devoted to Dissapation. It is of Brick (not elegant) & contains a Room for Dancing & two for Retirement and Cards." Fred Shelley (ed.), "The Journal of Ebenezer Hazard in Virginia, 1777," *Virginia Magazine of History and Biography*, LXII (1954), 403.

47. William Anderson, a successful merchant of Hanover County, Virginia, removed to Vauxhall, England, during the American Revolution. He continued as a merchant in London and acquired a considerable estate before his death in 1796. See copy of William Anderson's will in W. P. Anderson, *Anderson Family Records* (Cincinnati, 1936), pp. 10–11.

48. The sale of the indentures of "76 healthy indented SERVANTS, most of whom are are very useful Tradesmen, Farmers, Husbandmen, &c." was to commence on May 16. The *Planter* was to load with tobacco "in the Interest of Mr. *Samuel Gist.*" *Virginia Gazette*

(Purdie & Dixon), May 5, 1774. Samuel Gist was a storekeeper for John Smith, gentleman, a wealthy merchant of Hanover Town, Virginia. Shortly after Smith's death in 1746, Gist married his widow and established himself in London as a merchant in the Virginia trade. In 1768 his daughter Mary married Captain William Anderson. See "An act to vest the estate of Samuel Gist, in Mary the wife of William Anderson, and her heirs and assigns, and for other purposes" passed by the General Assembly of Virginia in 1782, in Hening, *Statutes*, XI, 54–55; and Eugenia G. & Preston G. Glazebrook (comps.), *Virginia Migrations: Hanover County* (2 vols., Richmond, 1944, 1949), II, 13 *et seq.*

49. Possibly Daniel McDonald of Stafford County, the son of the Rev. Daniel McDonald, minister of Brunswick Parish in King George County at the time of his death in 1762. The Rev. Daniel McDonald was born in County Antrim, Ireland. *Tyler's Quarterly Historical and Genealogical Magazine*, XXVIII (1947), 109–110; and King, *Register of Overwharton Parish*, p. 72. Peter Cooley, age 38, and his three sons, ages 18, 16, and 12, were weavers from London.

50. The Fredericksburg fair, established in 1738, seems to have been the most active and successful fair held in the colony. In 1769 the General Assembly designated that the fair be held "on the Monday next after the third Thursday in May and September annually." Hening, *Statutes*, V, 82–83; *ibid.*, VIII, 418–419.

51. Chopin, a Scottish unit of liquid capacity equal to half a Scottish pint or about an English quart.

52. The Fredericksburg May Fair purse of £50 was won by Moore Fauntleroy's bay mare Miss Alsop; the loser was William Fitzhugh's gray mare Kitty Fisher. *Virginia Gazette* (Purdie & Dixon), June 9, 1774. See Feb. 17, 1774, for a detailed description of the conditions and specifications for the race.

53. Harrower must have kept daily notes of his travels between December 6, 1773, and May 25, 1774. After purchasing the small notebook in Fredericksburg, he apparently copied the earlier journal. This notebook is undoubtedly the vellum-bound book that contains the manuscript journal. The religious volume is probably "THE *Christian's Daily Monitor,* on the Four Last Things, *viz.* DEATH, JUDGEMENT, HEAVEN, and HELL. Being an earnest Exhortation to a Holy Dying: With proper Directions in order to a Timely Repentance. Also suitable Prayers and Ejaculations for Sick Persons." This title was advertised in the *Virginia Gazette,* May 23, 1745, as just published by William Parks.

54. Edwin, born in 1766, inherited the mansion house Belvidera. Fredericksburg District Court Book E, 1803–1806, 346. He apparently led a rather dissolute life. When he died in 1842, Belvidera was sold by his creditors. Spotsylvania County Deed Book KK, 1842–1844, 105–107.

Bathurst, born May 29, 1767, became a sea captain. In 1795 he married Eliza Kay in Liverpool, England. In 1800 they settled in Alexandria, Virginia, where he commanded several vessels belonging to the port. He was appointed surveyor of the port of Alexandria by President Monroe and held that office until his death on February 22, 1827. F. L. Brockett, *The Lodge of Washington, A History of the Alexandria Washington Lodge No. 22, A. F. and A. M. of Alexandria, Va., 1783–1876* (Alexandria, 1876), p. 131.

William Allen, born October 13, 1769, received his education in medicine at Edinburgh and Paris. He first settled in Alexandria about 1800 but moved to his estate outside that city in Prince Georges County, Maryland, about 1806. He served in the War of 1812 as a colonel of the militia and died at his estate on October 19, 1821. *Ibid.,* p. 126.

Hannah Bassett, born in 1772, mar-

ried Samuel Moseley, a member of a prominent family of Princess Anne County. Her husband was an alderman of the City of Norfolk for many years and served as mayor of Norfolk in 1796 and 1797. *Lower Norfolk County Antiquary* (1897), I, p. 16. See deed of Samuel Moseley and Hannah Bassett, his wife, to Francis T. Brooke, dated August 30, 1796, in Spotsylvania County Deed Book O, 1794–1797, 401–404.

55. Snow Creek plantation in Caroline County was situated across Snow Creek from Belvidera. The creek formed the boundary between Spotsylvania and Caroline counties. The house was probably built by Mrs. Daingerfield's grandfather, Colonel John Taliaferro (1687–1744). *William and Mary Quarterly,* 1st ser., XVII (1908), 65. The mill was built about 1770. Colonel Daingerfield petitioned the court on June 4, 1770, for permission to erect a mill on Long Branch of Snow Creek. Spotsylvania County Order Book [Minutes], 1768–1770.

56. The news of the passage of the Boston Port Act appeared on May 19 in both Williamsburg newspapers. The resolution of the Burgesses designating June 1 "as a Day of Fasting, Humiliation, and Prayer" was passed on May 24. Two days later Governor Dunmore dissolved the House. Many Virginia parishes also appointed June 1 as a day of fasting. For an account of the church services at Fredericksburg, see *Virginia Gazette* (Purdie & Dixon), June 9, 1774.

57. John Glassell was a Scotsman who came to Fredericksburg and became a leading merchant there. He returned to Scotland at the beginning of the Revolution and purchased the estate of Long Middry, 16 miles from Edinburgh. His only daughter and heiress married Lord John Campbell, who became the Duke of Argyle. Horace Edwin Hayden (comp.), *Virginia Genealogies* (Baltimore, 1959), pp. 4–5.

58. The wright or carpenter, John

Pattie, resists all efforts at positive in-
dentification. In the Spotsylvania court
of June, 1772, John Pattie and Susan-
nah his wife are mentioned. Spotsylvania County Order Book [Minutes],
1768–1774. If he lived in Caroline
County, he may have been the John
Pattie who owned four slaves there in
1783, or he may have been a brother of
the James Pattie, a skilled weaver and
carpenter, who lived near Port Royal
in Caroline County. Tax List, Caroline
County, 1783, Archives Division, Virginia State Library; T. E. Campbell,
*Colonial Caroline: A History of Caro-
line County, Virginia* (Richmond,
1954), p. 407.

59. Thomas Evans lived in Caroline
County in the neighborhood of Belvidera. The inventory of his estate was
ordered recorded by the Caroline
County Court of July, 1795, but unfortunately the will and deed books
for the county have not survived.

60. Benjamin Edge was a planter in
Caroline County. He is recorded as
owning one slave in 1783. Tax List,
1783, Caroline County, Archives Division, Virginia State Library.

61. Colonel Daingerfield's use of a
scythe for harvesting wheat was not
typical. Throughout the colonial period wheat was harvested with the
sickle. In fact, the Englishman, J. F. D.
Smyth, claimed the distinction of in-
troducing the use of the scythe and the
cradle just after the Revolutionary
War. J. F. D. Smyth, *A Tour in the
United States . . .* (2 vols., London,
1784), II, 112–115; see also Gray, *Agriculture*, I, 170.

62. John Edge was the illegitimate
son of Samuel Edge of Caroline
County, the brother of Benjamin Edge.
Samuel Edge bequeathed much of his
property in trust to his son John
Edge alias Richeson. Much litigation
over the will and the estate followed
John's death about 1816. Edge vs.
Battaile, File 93, Fredericksburg Dis-
trict Court.

63. Since William Richards and his
wife were not indentured servants or
members of the family, they must have
been employed as skilled and probably
seasonal help at Belvidera. He could
have been a miller or a blacksmith,
while she could have been a seamstress,
a cook, or a nurse.

64. The "Taylor" may have been
Christopher Beck of Caroline County
with whom Harrower became quite
friendly. "Buckskin" was a nickname
for an American, especially a Virginian.

65. Probably Lewis Richards (1763–
1846), son of Philemon Richards of
Spotsylvania County. After the American Revolution father and son moved
to Kentucky.

66. Robert Forbes, a mason in Lerwick, requested on November 6, 1771,
from the Kirk Session of Lerwick a
loan of £5 Sterling "for which sum he
offered heritable security upon the
house presently possest by Elizabeth
Scott, his mother-in-law." "Annals of
Lerwick," *Shetland Times*, May 28,
1898.

67. A reference to the preceding page
of the manuscript journal.

68. Communication between Shetland and Scottish ports was at that
time infrequent and uncertain. The
Rev. John Mill noted in his diary that
news of the battle of Saratoga, fought
in October, 1777, reached him in February, 1778, and in 1790 his supply of
newspapers for six months reached
him at one time. Goudie, *Diary of the
Reverend John Mill*, p. xxxvii. Harrower not only mentions the lack of
shipping from Shetland during the
winter months, but he records the receipt on May 27, 1775, of a letter from
his wife dated March 1, 1775, in answer to his letter of June 14, 1774.
Patrick Neill early in the nineteenth
century noted: "The remote situation
of the Shetland Islands, and the little
intercourse they have, especially during winter, with the mother country,
frequently render the inhabitants
strangers for many weeks to the great-

est national occurences. It has often been alleged that the Revolution of 1688 was not known in Shetland for six months after it happened." Neill, *Tour of Orkney and Shetland*, p. 76.

69. Colonel Daingerfield's son John must have died at an early age. He is not included among the heirs of the estate.

70. Brooks was a carpenter for Colonel Alexander Spotswood of Nottingham. (See note 126, *infra*). It may have been this Thomas Brooks who, as an apprentice, caused Philemon Richards to be haled into court in 1772 to answer his complaints. Spotsylvania County Order Book [Minutes], 1768–1774, entry for July 16, 1772.

71. This "new machine" described by Harrower was invented by John Hobday of Gloucester County. On June 15, 1774, he was awarded a gold medal and a pecuniary reward for his "very ingenious and useful Machine" by the Society for the Advancement of Useful Knowledge. *Virginia Gazette* (Purdie & Dixon), June 16, 1774. The medal, bearing a reproduction of the machine, is preserved in the Virginia Historical Society. John Hobday announced on November 30, 1773, that he would set out on April 1 to instruct planters along the James and York rivers who were interested in erecting his machines. His brother Isaac was to go through the counties on the Rappahannock and Potomac rivers for the same purpose. The announcement included a list of materials needed for the machines. *Ibid.*, Dec. 2, 1773. Isaac Hobday probably directed the installation of the machine described by Harrower.

72. It was the practice in the cultivation of corn in colonial Virginia to pull fodder, i.e., to pull the tender leaves from the plant while still green and wrap them in bundles to be used as feed for livestock during the winter. It was also the practice to cut off the top of the stalk just above the highest ear and store the tops for fodder. Gray, *Agriculture*, I, 174.

73. Fredericksburg was a lively center of horse racing at this time. The October, 1774, races were arranged by the forty-four members of the Fredericksburg Jockey Club. The first day's race, the Jockey Club Plate, was open to members only. Its purse of 100 guineas was won by Regulus, a bay horse owned by William Fitzhugh of Chatham, Stafford County. The race on Wednesday, for a "Give and Take Purse" of £50, was won by a bay mare Single Peeper owned by Colonel John Tayloe of Mount Airy. The "Town Purse" of £50 was taken on Thursday by William Fitzhugh's gray mare Kitty Fisher. On Friday the "Town and Country Purse" of £50 was won by another Fitzhugh horse Volunteer, a chestnut gelding. It is interesting that all the races were won by horses owned by cousins, Fitzhugh and Tayloe. These wealthy gentlemen were noted horse fanciers. The October 20, 1774, issue of the *Virginia Gazette* (Purdie & Dixon) contains a complete summary of the races. The race horse Regulus is described and his accomplishments listed in *ibid.* (Purdie), April 19, 1776.

74. Harrower contradicted himself in regard to the amount of wheat sowed by Colonel Daingerfield. In the third letter to his wife, dated December 6, 1774, Harrower stated that 260 bushels were used. The latter amount is probably correct, because it was customary to plant at least half a bushel to an acre. Gray, *Agriculture*, I, 170. At Belvidera about 400 acres were planted in wheat each year.

75. The Rev. James Marye, Jr., studied at the College of William and Mary and was licensed as a minister for Virginia in 1755. After serving St. Thomas's Parish, Orange County, 1761–1768, he was selected by the vestry of St. George's Parish, Spotsylvania County, to succeed his deceased father. He served this parish until his death in 1780. The Rev. Edward Lewis Goodwin, *The Colonial Church in Virginia* (Milwaukee, 1927), p. 292; Carrol H. Quenzel, *The History and Background of St. George's Episco-*

pal Church, Fredericksburg, Virginia (Richmond, 1951), p. 16 *et seq.*

76. Captain James Craigie was a leading merchant of Lerwick. The Craigies of Stebbiegrind were prominent in affairs of the church and local government. At a meeting of the heritors of Lerwick on May 13, 1752, Captain Craigie was commissioned to send a small sloop to Leith for food to relieve the suffering in the parish. In 1763 he was appointed overseer and superintendent of the building of the new tolbooth in Lerwick. "Annals of Lerwick," *Shetland Times,* July 24, 1897. The parochial register of Lerwick records the marriage on March 17, 1755, of John Harrower and Ann Graeme, who has been identified as Captain Craigie's half-sister by Mr. John J. Graham, Lerwick. The Sasine Register at Edinburgh lists tenements held by "John Harrower merchant in Lerwick and Anna Graham his spouse" in 1762, 1767, and 1770. J. Franklin Jameson (ed.), "Diary of John Harrower, 1773–1776," *American Historical Review,* VI (1900), 66.

77. Possibly whisky, as differentiated from rum.

78. The battle of Point Pleasant, at the junction of the Kanawha and Ohio rivers, was the bloodiest engagement in Dunmore's War. Colonel Andrew Lewis was in command of the Virginia Militia during the battle; the Indians were led by Cornstalk of the Shawnee tribe. Harrower's information appears to have been drawn largely from the account in the *Virginia Gazette* (Pinkney), Nov. 10, 1774.

79. Virginians contributed generously to the relief of Boston. An anonymous person from Fredericksburg wrote on September 14, 1774: "Very liberal Contributions have been made, in this Place, for the Relief of the Poor in Boston. Mr. MANN PAGE, Jun. one of our Representatives, has taken uncommon Pains to promote the Subscriptions, and I dare say his most sanguine Expectations are fully answered." *Virginia Gazette* (Purdie & Dixon), Sept. 15, 1774.

80. The parochial registers of Lerwick record the births of the following children of John and Ann Harrower: John, born November 24, 1762; Elizabeth, born March 11, 1764; George, baptized March 12, 1766; and James, born July 18, 1767, died December 17, 1768. (Registers searched by the Scots Ancestry Research Society, Edinburgh.)

81. James Vance was one of the most esteemed men in Lerwick. A native of Queensferry, he apparently came to Lerwick in the customs service. In 1758 he was appointed postmaster. He became an active elder in the kirk, serving as session clerk, and then kirk treasurer. He took a great interest in education, bequeathing a legacy to the Society for Propagating Christian Knowledge to assist in establishing a school in Lerwick. His second wife was Barbara Craigie, a cousin of Ann Harrower. "Annals of Lerwick," *Shetland Times,* May 22, 1897.

82. William Ferguson, a native of Thurso in Caithness, was supervisor of excise at Lerwick. His wife was Ann Ross, sister of Margaret Ross, the wife of James Craigie.

83. Deall is a small village a short distance north of Lerwick. Harrower's connection with Deall is not clear, but Mr. John Stewart, Aberdeen, writes that Ann Harrower's sisters married in that area.

84. Lucy Gaines, the housekeeper at Belvidera, was probably the daughter of Robert and Ursula Gaines. Her father died intestate in Spotsylvania County in 1763. Her sister Alice seems to have married John Robinson of the Wilderness section of lower Orange County. See also entries of February 4, 1776 and April 12, 1776. No information has been found about Lucy Gaines after she left Belvidera on July 23, 1776.

85. Christopher Beck, tailor, was living in Caroline County in 1760 when the court assigned an apprentice to him. He appears also in the Caroline County tax list of 1783.

86. For advertisements of Porter's

mercantile business, see *Virginia Gazette* (Rind), June 16, 1774; (Purdie & Dixon), Dec. 1, 1774; (Dixon & Hunter), Nov. 8, 1776. He was named to the Committee of Correspondence for the town on June 1, 1774. He owned a plantation of 400 acres in Spotsylvania seven miles from Fredericksburg, which he advertised for sale in 1780. *Ibid.* (Dixon & Nicholson), March 18, 1780. When he became insane in 1786 his son, William Porter, Jr., Harrower's pupil, assumed responsibility for the business. American Loyalist Claims Commission, P.R.O., T. 79/92, 180–181; see also the records of a suit over the estate of William Porter, Sr., Farish vs. Porter, File No. 107, Fredericksburg District Court.

87. Captain John Lurtey of King George County married Rose Bronough, daughter of David Bronough, gentleman. He died in 1795 and his will is recorded in King George County Will Book No. 2, 1780–1804, 195.

88. After he left Daingerfield's employ, Anthony Frazer (1754–1804) became an officer in the Continental Army, deputy sheriff in Spotsylvania County, and clerk of the vestry of St. George's Parish. He married Hannah Herndon in 1780, and when he died of consumption on March 4, 1804, he had a substantial estate, a large family, and an enviable reputation as "a gentleman much esteemed by his neighbours and acquaintances." Francis B. Heitman (comp.), *Historical Register of Officers of the Continental Army* (Washington, 1914), p. 236; St. George's Parish Vestry Book (Ms. in Alderman Library, University of Virginia); Tax Lists of Spotsylvania County, 1782, in the Archives Division, Virginia State Library; *Virginia Herald and Fredericksburg Advertiser*, March 9, 1804.

89. An announcement of the death of Mrs. Priscilla Dawson of Williamsburg "at the house of Mr. William Daingerfield near Fredericksburg" appeared in the *Virginia Gazette* (Pur-

die), March 24, 1775. Mrs. Dawson, the daughter of William Bassett of Eltham, was Colonel Daingerfield's first cousin. She was the widow of the Rev. Thomas Dawson, Commissary to the Bishop of London, member of the Council, and President of the College of William and Mary. The daughter was probably Rebecca, whose birth was mentioned in a letter of Dawson to Lady Gooch, January 11, 1758. *William and Mary Quarterly*, 2nd ser., I (1921), 52–53.

90. Perhaps the Martin Heeley who was engaged in recruiting ten men in 1778 so as to receive an ensign's commission in the battalion of infantry being raised for garrison duty. H. R. McIlwaine and Wilmer L. Hall (eds.), *Journals of the Council of the State of Virginia* (3 vols., Richmond, 1931–1952), II, 89, 154. A Martin Heeley was initiated into the Williamsburg Lodge of Freemasons on June 19, 1778. George Eldridge Kidd, *Early Freemasonry in Williamsburg, Virginia* (Richmond, 1957), p. 74. The wedding of Martin Heely and Mrs. Mary Burgess, widow, occurred in Norfolk County on January 12, 1784. *William and Mary Quarterly*, 2nd series, VIII (1928), 169.

91. John McDearman (or McDearmand) apparently was an overseer for Colonel Daingerfield at the Snow Creek plantation; see entry of July 22, 1775.

92. Colonel Mann Page (1718–1781) of Mannsfield, Spotsylvania County, was born at Rosewell, Gloucester County. After graduating from the College of William and Mary, he moved to Spotsylvania County. About 1765 he built Mannsfield midway between Belvidera and Fredericksburg. It was a handsome house fashioned after Mount Airy, the home of his second wife, Ann Corbin Tayloe. He was a justice of the peace of Spotsylvania County, a vestryman of St. George's Parish, one of the commissioners of the Fredericksburg Gun Factory during the Revolution, and a delegate to the Continental Congress in 1777.

93. The Rev. Francis Wilson, minister of Drysdale Parish, Caroline County.

94. Sally Pettin, who was "brought up and raised" by Edge. See copy of Samuel Edge's will proved at Caroline County Court, Jan. 10, 1788, in Edge vs. Battaile, File 93, Fredericksburg District Court.

95. Mr. Hugh Tracey, Director of the International Library of African Music, Transvaal, Union of South Africa, identifies the instrument as a "ballafon," one of the many types of xylophone found in Africa. It would now be called a marimba "and would have been resonated by an oblong box, the notes being supported on the two sides of the box."

96. The Rev. Abner Waugh (1738–1806) of St. Mary's Parish, Caroline County. After attending the College of William and Mary from 1765 to 1768, he studied theology and was licensed for Virginia in 1771. He succeeded the Rev. Jonathan Boucher at Mount Church, St. Mary's Parish. Loyal to the American cause during the Revolution, he served on the committee of Safety of Caroline County and as a chaplain for the Second Virginia Regiment, 1775–1776. In 1788 he was named chaplain for the Virginia Convention which ratified the Federal Constitution. He died shortly after leaving St. Mary's to become rector of St. George's Parish in 1806. Bishop William Meade, *Old Churches, Ministers and Families of Virginia* (2 vols.), Philadelphia, n.d.), I, 410–412; *Virginia Magazine of History and Biography*, XLI (1933), 303; Campbell, *Colonial Caroline*, p. 245 et seq.; and King, *Register of Overwharton Parish*, p. 244.

97. Harrower had difficulty collecting the money owed him for teaching. Samuel Edge was particularly troublesome.

98. Probably Thomas Anderson, a shoemaker in Fredericksburg. See journal entries of May 27, 1775 and August 10, 1775.

99. John Mitchell, Culpeper County, owned 100 acres in 1782. Land Tax

Records of Caroline County, 1782, Archives Division, Virginia State Library.

100. Colonel John Tayloe Corbin (c. 1745–1794) of Laneville in King and Queen County. Corbin also had a quarter at Moss Neck in Caroline County. He was the son of Richard Corbin, Receiver-General of the Colony of Virginia. From 1769 through 1774 he represented King and Queen County in the House of Burgesses. In 1771 he married Maria Waller, daughter of Benjamin Waller of Williamsburg.

101. A checkerboard.

102. First reports of the engagements at Lexington and Concord reached Williamsburg on April 29. Two express riders reached the capital on the same day. The first account mentioned only Lexington, but the second rider carried a brief note concerning both Lexington and Concord, as well as the repulse of the British. *Virginia Gazette* (Dixon & Hunter), April 29, 1775. Harrower apparently heard the news from the second express rider.

103. The secret removal of gunpowder from the Public Magazine in Williamsburg during the night of April 20–21, 1775, by order of Governor Dunmore greatly angered the Virginians. Fredericksburg was the principal assembly point for the militia. *Virginia Gazette* (Purdie), April 28, May 12, 1775; also *ibid.* (Dixon & Hunter), April 29, May 13, 1775.

104. James Brown was for many years a silversmith in Fredericksburg. George B. Cutten, *The Silversmiths of Virginia* (Richmond, 1952), pp. 37–38.

105. "TO BE SOLD in the upper End of *New Kent* County, a valuable Tract of LAND containing 1650 Acres, with a good Dwelling-House and all convenient Outhouses, on a beautiful and healthy Situation, the one Half of the Land first and second low Grounds, the latter capable of making extensive Meadows, but at present under a Growth of valuable Timber, such as Cypress, white Oak, Ash, and sweet Gum, and lying four Miles above the present Navigation of *Chickahominy*,

which will be extended considerably, as there are Subscriptions for the Purpose. I will sell Stocks of all Sorts, with or without the Land, also Corn, Fodder, and Wheat. Twenty Hands may be worked to Advantage on the above Land; and *John Miller*, who lives on the Premises, will shew it, and make known the Terms. I purpose selling my Land on *Pamunkey* River, below *Cumberland* Town, at *New Kent April* Court, and will lay it off in Lots of three or four Hundred Acres. WILLIAM DAINGERFIELD." *Virginia Gazette* (Dixon & Hunter), Dec. 5, 1777.

106. James Fulton advertised in March, 1769, that he operated a tailor shop in Fredericksburg "next door to Mr. *Benjamin Johnston's* (known by the name of the *Long Ordinary*)," and invited gentlemen "to favour him with their custom." His business must have prospered; two years later he offered employment to journeymen tailors. *Virginia Gazette* (Rind), April 27, 1769, and June 20, 1771.

107. Mr. and Mrs. William Porter. The "high school" may have been Mr. John Low's grammar school. In 1780, Mr. Low advertised that he had been teaching for eight years in Virginia "and had near two hundred pupils under his tuition." *Virginia Gazette* (Dixon & Nicolson), Richmond, Dec. 2, 1780. See *Virginia Magazine of History and Biography*, XXIX (1921), 102–105 for biographical sketch of John Low or Lowe (1750–1798).

108. St. John's Day.

109. James Craigie married Margaret, a daughter of John Ross of Lund, in 1759. Miss Peggy was probably Margaret, the younger daughter. The two sons were John of Strom, who later became a captain in the 47th Regiment, and William Thomas, who became a merchant in Leith. Francis J. Grant, *Zetland Family Histories* (Lerwick, 1907), p. 52.

110. The Rev. James Sands (1742–1805), minister of Lerwick, 1767–93, and of Tingwall, 1793–1803, married

Elizabeth, the sister of James Craigie and Ann Harrower. *Ibid.*, p. 51.

111. Henry Mitchell resided in Fredericksburg for many years before the Revolution. He was first a factor for McCall Smellie and Co., and then a partner in the firm of George McCall and Co. In March, 1775, Henry Mitchell came to the attention of the Orange County Committee of Safety through the ownership of several pamphlets "containing very obnoxious reflections on the Continental Congress." *Virginia Gazette* (Dixon & Hunter), April 15, 1775. The subcommittee for Spotsylvania County, on July 15, 1776, summoned Mitchell and ten other merchants to appear and take the oath of allegiance specified by the May Convention. When they refused, the committee declared them inimical to America and ordered them disarmed. *Ibid.* (Purdie), Aug. 23, 1776. Early in 1777, Mitchell announced his intention to leave the country and offered his houses and lots for sale or rent. *Ibid.* (Purdie), Feb. 28, 1777. He left Fredericksburg shortly after this announcement but returned about 1785 and died there in 1793. American Loyalist Claims Commission, P.R.O., T. 79/91, 163–164; Henry Mitchell's will is recorded in Fredericksburg Hustings Court Will Book A, 1782–1807, 138–139.

112. Harrower's family apparently moved from Twageos to cheaper quarters in Lerwick.

113. On the west of the island of Mainland, about ten miles from Lerwick. Mr. John J. Graham, suggests that John was in Walls to attend the school of George Greig, a very capable teacher. There was no parochial school in Lerwick and several parents sent their children to Walls.

114. The Wallers of Spotsylvania County were a numerous clan. "Old Mrs. Waller" may have been Mary Pendleton Waller (1720–1808), widow of the Clerk of Spotsylvania, Edmund Waller; Agnes Carr Waller (1712–

1779), wife of John Waller; or Elizabeth Dabney Waller (c. 1705–1794), widow of Thomas Waller. This list does not exhaust the possibilities. *Virginia Magazine of History and Biography*, LIX (1951), 337–352.

115. John Dalton, tailor, his wife Elizabeth, and their son Walker leased a house and lot in Fredericksburg from Pearson Chapman of Maryland in 1768. In 1779 he sold his lease to John Welch, a cooper, and moved to Petersburg where he died insolvent. Crozier, *Spotsylvania County*, pp. 350, 443. A contemporary summarized his career briefly: "At his first commencement of business in Fredericksburg he was thought to be in prosperous circumstances but before he left it, he had taken to hard Drink and his affairs rapidly declined." American Loyalist Claims Commission, P.R.O., T. 79/93, 21. The identity of the unfortunate Mary Fitzgerald could not be determined.

116. Possibly William Payne, a clerk and bookkeeper and a fellow passenger on the *Planter*. Did Mr. Anderson also persuade Payne to take a position as a tutor?

117. Colonel William Daingerfield was related through his mother, Hannah Bassett, with Mrs. Martha Washington. The Hon. Burwell Bassett of Eltham, Colonel Daingerfield's first cousin, married Anna Maria Dandridge, and her sister Martha married George Washington. In addition to Mrs. Washington, the party included John Parke Custis (1755–1781) and his wife Eleanor Calvert; Mrs. Spotswood was Elizabeth Washington (1749–1814), the wife of Alexander Spotswood and a half-niece of General George Washington; Mrs. Campbell was Mary Dandridge, first cousin of Martha Washington and wife successively of Colonel John Spotswood, son of the governor, and John Campbell, who left her and went to the West Indies in 1767; Mrs. Dansie, whose maiden name was Ann Dandridge, was a sister of Mrs. Campbell and widow

of Captain Thomas Dansie; Miss Washington must have been a niece of General Washington; and the Miss Dandridge was, perhaps, Anne Dandridge, a niece of Mrs. Washington.

118. Mary White was the daughter of George and Anne Doniphan White of King George County. Molly White's great-aunt, Elizabeth Doniphan, married Stephen Hansford (1699–1772) of King George County. King, *Register of Overwharton Parish*, pp. 48, 129; *Tyler's Quarterly Historical and Genealogical Magazine*, XXVI (1945), 277–285.

119. Sucky is listed among the slaves in the inventory of Colonel Daingerfield's estate. Other slaves appearing in the inventory are Barnaby, mentioned in the entry for January 1, 1776; Ganzera [Gant Sarah] and Patty on February 23, 1776; Abraham [Abram] on February 27, 1776; and Jacob on May 31, 1776. Spotsylvania County Will Book E, 1772–1798, 590.

120. An ordinance of the Virginia Convention of July, 1775, had provided for the establishment of defense forces for the colony. In addition to regulars, the ordinance divided the colony into sixteen districts for raising minutemen from the militia. The battalion of minutemen of the district composed of Spotsylvania, Caroline, Stafford, and King George counties was to number five hundred rank and file divided into ten companies of fifty men each. Each battalion as soon as raised was to train twenty days, and also twelve days twice a year thereafter. Hening, *Statutes*, IX, 16–21.

121. Hazel Run, now in Fredericksburg, in 1776 was about a mile out of town. Wading a stream in December must have been most uncomfortable.

122. Perhaps the Daniel Dempsey who was ordered to be added to the list of tithables by the Orange County Court on August 26, 1756. Orange County Order Book No. 6, 1754–1763, 246.

123. Alexander Reid in 1767 was a gardener for Robert Page of Broadneck

in Hanover County. *Virginia Gazette* (Purdie & Dixon), July 30, 1767. When Robert Page died in 1768, Reid found employment with Robert's brother, Mann Page. Allason Papers, Ledger 2, 188, Archives Division, Virginia State Library.

124. Scott engraved currency for the Commonwealth of Virginia and in 1780 received £2,103/8/ for "Services & expences in detectg. some persons concerned in counterfeitg. the paper currency." McIlwaine and Hall, *Journals of the Council of the State of Virginia*, II, 257. In 1781 he moved to Philadelphia and advertised in the *Pennsylvania Packet*, May 27, 1781, as late engraver for the State of Virginia. On November 23, 1793, he was appointed engraver for the newly established mint in Philadelphia and was still holding this post in 1806. Cutten, *Silversmiths of Virginia*, p. 41.

125. Elizabeth Foster, daughter of Sheriff Anthony Foster, married James Frazer, the only child of William Frazer, about 1752. William, a native of Scotland, was a tailor and protegé of Governor Spotswood. Settling first at Germanna, he moved to Fredericksburg shortly after the establishment of the town in 1727. James and Elizabeth Frazer had six children of whom Anthony was the eldest. *Tyler's Quarterly Historical and Genealogical Magazine*, XXI (1940), 259–260.

126. Alexander Spotswood was the grandson of Governor Alexander Spotswood. His home Nottingham, built after his marriage in 1769, was described by Von Closen as "a charming residence near New Post, which is 4 miles from Fredericksburg." Evelyn M. Acomb (trans. & ed.), *The Revolutionary Journal of Baron Ludwig von Closen, 1780–1783* (Chapel Hill, 1958), p. 211. Spotswood entered the service in June, 1775, as a major of the Second Virginia Regiment. He advanced rapidly. On February 21, 1777, he was appointed a full colonel, but resigned on October 9 of that year. In the next year he attempted to regain his commission but was unsuccessful.

Early in 1781 he proposed the organization of two legions for the defense of the state and was named by the Assembly a brigadier general to command the troops. It was impossible to raise the necessary men and the legions never did go into service. Clayton Torrence, "A Cloud-Capped Legion," *William and Mary Quarterly*, 2nd series, I (1921), 137–141.

127. John Robinson of Orange County served as an ensign in the Revolution. He married Alice, daughter of Robert and Ursula Gaines.

128. John Frazer (c. 1756–1793) served with the Spotsylvania County militia during the Revolution. On February 21, 1782, he was recommended as a lieutenant in Captain Legg's Company. Spotsylvania County Order Book [Minutes], 1774–1782, 175. After the Revolution, John Frazer moved to Fredericksburg where he kept a tavern "at the sign of the GOLDEN EAGLE" until his death in 1793. The tavern, now called the Rising Sun, is preserved by the Association for the Preservation of Virginia Antiquities. *Tyler's Quarterly Historical and Genealogical Magazine*, XXI (1940), 260–261; *Virginia Herald and Fredericksburg Advertiser*, Sept. 27, 1792.

129. Mr. Jervis may have been James Jarvis who married Mary, the widow of William Brown, and in 1772 agreed to apprentice his stepson James to James Brown, a silversmith of Fredericksburg. Crozier, *Spotsylvania County*, p. 292. James Jarvis was appointed constable of Spotsylvania County on February 19, 1779. Spotsylvania County Order Book [Minutes], 1774–1782, 108.

130. Robert Johnston (c. 1730–1780) was a well-to-do merchant in Port Royal, Caroline County. During the Revolution he imported goods into Caroline from Philadelphia but ran afoul of the Caroline Committee of Safety for profiteering. When asked to reduce his prices to the pre-1775 level, he refused and withdrew his Philadelphia goods from the market. He then replenished his stock with merchandise imported from the non-British

West Indies. These goods he sold at advanced prices until the Committee again took action against him for "breaking the rules of the Association." Shortages of merchandise came to Johnston's aid and the matter ended amicably with a compromise. Campbell, *Caroline County*, p. 239.

131. Colonel Daingerfield must have purchased Ariel from Robert Slaughter (1748–1832) of the Grange, Culpeper County. The horse ran sixth out of eight entries in the first heat and was distanced in the second heat of the Fredericksburg race on October 5, 1774. Two days later Ariel was distanced in the first heat. *Virginia Gazette* (Purdie & Dixon), Oct. 20, 1774.

132. Probably one of the sons of Henry Rains of Drysdale Parish, Caroline County. In his will, proved February 12, 1767, in Caroline County Court, Henry Rains divided his plantation of 1,200 acres equally among his four sons John, Ambrose, Ignatius, and Henry. In a deed dated December 11, 1775, but not proved until June 12, 1794, Dr. John Rains of Philadelphia sold his share to Henry Hill of Philadelphia. The deed was witnessed by an array of worthies including Thomas Nelson, Jr., Richard Henry Lee, Francis Lightfoot Lee, Thomas Jefferson, and George Wythe. The land, as described in 1794, was up Snow Creek adjoining land of Molly and John Edge, and Gen. Alexander Spotswood, and thus near Belvidera. Loose Papers, Fredericksburg District Court.

133. John McCalley of St. George's Parish, Spotsylvania County. In his will, dated January 19, 1783, John McCalley mentions his wife Elizabeth; three sons Archibald, Charles, and James; and three daughters Ann, Elizabeth, and Mary. Spotsylvania County Will Book E, 1772–1798, 521. On December 21, 1780 the Spotsylvania County Court certified John McCalley's account for repairs to the Fredericksburg Warehouse, and in the March, 1781, court he was commissioned as a captain in the Spotsylvania militia. Spotsylvania County Order

Book [Minutes], 1774–1782, 151, 155.

134. Although Harrower identifies his friend as Thomas Miles (see entry July 28, 1776), no record has been found of him.

135. Joseph Jones (1727–1805) of King George County was an eminent statesman and jurist. Where he received his early education is unknown, but he was admitted to the Inner Temple in 1749, to the Middle Temple in May, 1751, and to the English bar in June, 1751. He returned to Virginia and in 1754 became deputy attorney for the king. In 1758 he married Mrs. Daingerfield's aunt Mary Taliaferro, daughter of Colonel John Taliaferro of Snow Creek. Elected first to the House of Burgesses in 1772, Jones served continuously in that House, in all of the Revolutionary conventions, and subsequently in the House of Delegates. He was chairman of the Committee of Safety for King George County in 1774 and subsequently was a member of the second Virginia Committee of Safety. In the Convention of 1776, Jones was an active member of the committee that framed the Virginia Declaration of Rights and the State Constitution. After being elected to the Continental Congress in 1777, he withdrew on January 23, 1778, upon his appointment as a judge of the Virginia General Court but resigned in less than two years to return to the Congress from 1780 to 1783. In 1789 he was reappointed judge of the General Court and continued in this office until his death in 1805. Joseph Jones was a friend of George Washington, a correspondent and partisan of Thomas Jefferson, an intimate colleague of James Madison, and had great influence over his (Jones's) nephew James Monroe. *Dictionary of American Biography*, X, 192–193; E. Alfred Jones, *American Members of the Inns of Court* (London, 1924), pp. 107–108; W. C. Ford (ed.), *Letters of Joseph Jones* (Washington, 1889).

136. The Virginia Convention of July, 1775, passed an ordinance establishing "a manufactory of arms ... at or

near Fredericksburg" under the direction of Fielding Lewis, Charles Dick, Mann Page, Jr., William Fitzhugh, and Samuel Selden, or any three of them. Hening, *Statutes*, IX, 71–73. Only Fielding Lewis and Charles Dick appear to have been active. An initial appropriation of £2,500 was made by the Convention. A tract of land adjoining Fredericksburg was purchased from Richard Brooke, the necessary buildings erected, and workmen hired. Charles Dick reported that he and Colonel Lewis accomplished the establishment of the factory during the first year "after much Trouble and Attention" and succeeded in putting it "on an extraordinary good footing." *William and Mary Quarterly*, 1st series, XXVII (1927), 248–257. The success of the arms factory was attested by Ebenezer Hazard when he visited it on May 28, 1777: "Went to see the Gunnery, as it is called, of which Mr. Dick is one of the Overseers. About 20 Musquets, complete with Bayonets, are made here in a Week. About 60 persons are employed, who have made all their own Tools, & do their Business with great Regularity & Expedition. They labour under some Difficulty for Want of proper Streams of Water, which encreases manual Labour & makes the Manufactory more expensive. The Musquets made here are excellent, lighter than the English, carry an Ounce Ball, & cost the Manufacturer about £4.10–Virga. Curry. or 15 Dollars. The Bayonets are 20 Ins. in Length." *Virginia Magazine of History and Biography*, LXII (1954), 404.

137. These were some of the Tory prisoners taken at the Battle of Moore's Creek Bridge, North Carolina, on February 27, 1776. The Tory forces, nearly all Scottish Highlanders, were disastrously defeated by Colonel James Moore's minutemen and militia; nearly eight hundred and fifty rank and file and thirty officers were made prisoners. In the list of prisoners are many Highland names. Force, *American Archives: Fourth Series*, V, 63.

138. On March 16, 1776 the Congress adopted a resolution designating May 17, 1776, "as a day of humiliation, fasting, and prayer" in all the colonies. W. C. Ford (ed.), *Journals of the Continental Congress, 1774–1789* (34 vols., Washington, 1904–1937), IV, 208–209.

139. Captain Anthony Strother (1736–1790) of Albion, King George County. His home was across the Rappahannock River from Belvidera.

140. Mrs. Lawrence Battaile of Prospect Hill, Caroline County. Her husband died in 1773. The two daughters taught by Harrower were Sarah Ryng Battaile who married an attorney, Thomas Reade Rootes of Gloucester County and Federal Hill, Fredericksburg, and Elizabeth Battaile, who married William Catesby Woodford of White Hall, Caroline County.

141. Mrs. Morton was probably a Mrs. Martin. The Martins settled early in Albermarle County. It is believed that Captain Joseph Martin, who died in 1761, came originally from Essex County, and this may explain the relationship between the widow and the Daingerfields. Rev. Edgar Woods, *Albermarle County in Virginia* (Bridgewater, Va., n.d.), pp. 263–265.

142. Jacob Whitley (1728–1789) was "for many years a very reputable innholder" in Fredericksburg. *Virginia Herald and Fredericksburg Advertiser*, Sept. 10, 1789. His inn stood on lots 35 and 36. Crozier, *Spotsylvania County*, 280–281. At his death in 1789, Whitley left "a moderate personal Estate and some valuable lots in Fredericksburg." American Loyalist Claims Commission, P.R.O., T. 79/93, 28.

143. Mary Sullivan, an innkeeper in Fredericksburg.

144. The only Harbin Moore living at this time was a well-known planter in Culpeper County. No evidence could be found that Moore owned a quarter in Caroline County, but Harrower indicated that he lived between Prospect Hill and Belvidera.

145. The Virginia Convention of

December 1775 authorized the Committee of Safety "to provide from time to time such and so many armed vessels as they may judge necessary for the protection of the several rivers in this colony." Hening, *Statutes*, IX, 83. The Committee of Safety ordered immediately the construction of two row galleys for the protection of each of the principal rivers and the Eastern Shore in Virginia. See letter of George Mason and John Dalton to the Maryland Council of Safety, Jan. 31, 1776, in Kate Mason Rowland, *The Life of George Mason 1725–1792* (2 vols., New York, 1892), I, 214. Colonel Fielding Lewis of Fredericksburg was in charge of the shipyard on the Rappahannock. On June 7, 1776, Caleb Herbert was engaged as the "Master Builder for the Ship Yard." The two row galleys, the *Lewis* and the *Page*, were completed by the fall of 1776. Navy Board Letter Book, 1776–1777, Archives Division, Virginia State Library; McIlwaine and Hall, *Journals of the Council of the State of Virginia*, I, 7.

146. Perhaps John Wright (1734–1791) of Spotsylvania County and William Bruce (c. 1724–1792) of King George County, who were related by marriage. Mr. Wright was an inspector of tobacco at his death. King, *Register of Overwharton Parish*, p. 135.

147. James Frazer of Red House, Spotsylvania County, had a distinguished Revolutionary War record. His horse Rainbow was killed under him at the Battle of Cowpens and he was present at the Siege of Yorktown. He died in 1799. *Tyler's Quarterly Historical and Genealogical Magazine*, XXI (1940), 261.

148. This information from Fredericksburg was reported in the *Virginia Gazette* (Purdie), July 12, 1776: "The postmaster in Fredericksburg writes, of last Wednesday, that, by a gentleman just arrived from Philadelphia, he had seen an Evening Post of the 2d instant, which mentions that the Hon. the Continental Congress had that day declared the *United Colonies free and independent states*."

149. Harrower was probably removing lead from the Snow Creek house for military purposes. Scarcity of lead during the Revolution was a serious problem in Virginia. Charles Dick of Fredericksburg wrote to Colonel George Muter on September 5, 1780 complaining of the shortage of lead at the Gunnery: "There is no Lead to be bought, and none this way belonging to the public." He also mentioned that "the Leads of our Windows & Shop Weights are already gone." Palmer, *Calendar of Virginia State Papers*, I, 372.

INDEX

Index